Indigenous Educational Models for Contemporary Practice

In Our Mother's Voice

Edited by

Maenette Kape'ahiokalani Padeken Ah Nee-Benham
Michigan State University

With

Joanne Elizabeth Cooper
University of Hawai'i, Mānoa

 LAWRENCE ERLBAUM ASSOCIATES, PUBLISHERS

2000   Mahwah, New Jersey   London

Lawrence Erlbaum Associates, Inc., Publishers
10 Industrial Avenue
Mahwah, New Jersey 07430-2262

Cover design by Kathryn Houghtaling Lacey

Library of Congress Cataloging-in-Publication Data

Indigenous educational models for contemporary practice : in our
mother's voice / edited by Maenette Kapeàhiokalani Padeken Ah
Nee-Benham with Joanne Elizabeth Cooper.
    p. cm.— (Sociocultural, political,a nd historical studies in education)

    Includes bibliographical references and index.

  ISBN 0-8058-3461-3 (cloth : alk. paper) —
0-8058-3462-1 (pbk : alk. paper)
  1. Indigenous peoples—Education—Social Case studies. 2. Native
language and education—Case studies. I. Nee-Benham, Maenette
K. P. II. Cooper, Joanne E. III. Series.

LC3719.I53 2000
371.829'97—dc21

                                                        99-059724
                                                        CIP

Printed in the United States of America
10 9 8 7 6 5 4 3 2 1

*In memory of Ingrid Washinawatok who devoted
her life to indigenous people.
To our native children and youth, today and
seven generations hence.*

*Hoe aku i kou wa'a!
(Paddle your canoe forward!)*

Contents

From the Series Editor

Joel Spring
Choctaw

Indigenous Educational Models for Contemporary Practice: In Our Mother's Voice gives meaning to Article 15 of the United Nations' Draft Declaration of Indigenous Peoples Rights. The Declaration proclaims:

> Indigenous children have the right to all levels and forms of education of the State. All indigenous peoples also have this right and the right to establish and control their educational systems and institutions providing education in their own languages, in a manner appropriate to their cultural methods of teaching and learning.[1]

The legacy of colonialism and genocide has made it difficult to fulfill this right. Many educational traditions and practices have been lost or only remain in the memories of survivors of the indigenous peoples' holocaust. This volume restores this educational legacy and adapts it to the reality of the global economy and culture. Furthermore, this book does more than recapture a lost past. The educational models included in this volume affirm the vitality of these traditions and their adaptability to contemporary times.

In a broader context, the world's people should pay close attention to indigenous educational models as alternatives to current global standards that link economic development to educational practices. These dominant models focused on training workers for an economic system that produces environmental destruction, unhappiness, and an empty spirit. Speaking before the United Nations in 1992, Thomas Banyacya, last of the four Hopi messengers sent by the Great Spirit Maasau'u, Guardian of the Earth, to warn that the earth was out of balance and headed for destruction, described a rock drawing found in Hopiland that shows part of the Hopi prophecy. There are two paths. The first, with high technology but separate from natural and spiritual law, leads to jagged lines that represent chaos. The lower path remains in harmony with natural law. Here we see a line that represents a choice like a bridge joining the paths. If we return to spiritual harmony and live from our hearts we can experience a paradise in this world. If we continue only on this upper path, we will come to destruction.[2]

It is my hope and belief that the educational models described in this book will help put students, teachers, and the world on a path to harmony and hope. In closing, I offer the following gift to the spirit of this book:

Cleansing the Blood of My Ancestors
My father's father and his father's father were all chiefs
but not the type that brought good to their people.
Born from the joining of a Frenchman and Pushmataha's daughters
they preached that forgetting the old ways would end the genocide
but they were wrong.
One signed a treaty of destruction,
another built schools to teach English—of all things, Latin and Greek.
Forget the old ways, they proclaimed,
forget your mother's tongue,
forget the stories of tribal birth and of your links to the scared hoop of life,
forget it all.
we now have a better way to teach and learn,
this new way will make you rich and strong.
But the riches turned out to be mere paper and coin,
poor sustenance for those seeking joy and life.
The strength turned out to be power to destroy,
to destroy mother earth.
So now I must cleanse my ancestors blood,
restore the lost good.
I must find the lost ways of teaching
because what we have now has surely failed.

ENDNOTES

1. The "United Nations Draft Declaration of Human Rights" may be found in Alexander Ewen, *Voice of Indigenous Peoples* (Santa Fe, New Mexico: Clear Light Publishers, 1994), p. 166.
2. Thomas Banyacya, *The Hopi Message to the United Nations General Assembly,* http:www.alphacde.com/banyacya/un92.html (February 15, 1999), pp. 4–5.

Foreword

Valorie Johnson
Cayuga-Seneca

As is customary in most Iroquois gatherings, the words that come before all else are those of giving thanks for all the gifts of life. They are usually given in the form of the Thanksgiving Address, which can often take several hours to recite. This ancient message of peace and appreciation of Mother Earth is an acknowledgment of the full circle of creation. As a tradition that is hundreds of years old, the Address is given to help us, as human beings, put our minds together as one, and learn to live in peace and harmony with one another and with Mother Earth.

So it is with that same spirit that I begin the Foreword for this book. First, I acknowledge all the gifts that have been given to human beings by the Creator, such as the water, plants, animals, stars, and all the other wonders of nature. I give thanks to those ancestors who struggled, often against great odds, to hold tightly to their beliefs that the natural world is a precious and rare gift for which we must always be thankful. They are the ones who recognized that these gifts have sustained us and made us strong, and that as human beings, we have responsibilities to protect these gifts of which we are a part. They are the ancestors who fought many types of battles to maintain the land and keep our cultures alive. They are my ancestors ... and they are also the ancestors of many indigenous peoples around the world.

Like the Iroquois, there are many indigenous peoples who have evolved cultures over many centuries that are based on a delicate balance between their needs and those of nature. Yet, in past centuries for some groups and in decades for others, many indigenous peoples have suffered from the conse-quences of vast, destructive development and colonization. Not only have indigenous societies often been forced from traditional homelands, they have also been forced to endure other atrocities that have destroyed the lives of far too many individuals. As a result, today indigenous peoples are among the most economically disadvantaged groups in society, suffering the worst health, receiving the least education and are among the poorest.

Today, there are more than 250 million indigenous peoples and the pop-ulations are rapidly growing. At the edge of the millennium, we find many indigenous groups that are fighting for survival. They are demanding the re-turn of their lands, the end of colonization, control of the education of their children, and the right to be self-determining regarding their own futures and living by their own cultural ways.

Most important, many indigenous cultures continue to survive, or, are being revitalized. Many groups recognize that traditional indigenous knowledge and thought holds critical answers for some contemporary soci-etal issues. For example, as others in the world see the destruction of the rivers and rainforests and their negative effects, they recognize that the sur-vival of humankind depends on the survival of Earth. Furthermore, they of-ten realize that the framework for future development, referred to as *sustainability*, was always an integral part of most indigenous cultures. As in-digenous cultures grow in strength, it is predicted that there will continue to be other answers that will help ensure the survival of Earth, and us.

So it is that I continue to give thanks. I thank the Creator for the incredi-ble individuals who were involved in this particular effort. Like many of our ancestors were in their lifetimes, the educators at this gathering represented the ones who assumed their responsibilities to care for the next seven gener-ations. They are the ones who, throughout their lives, have fought the tough battles to perpetuate traditional Native knowledge and develop edu-cation that, in turn, develops indigenous youth into "whole" human beings. In their own ways, each is recognized by members of their community as a strong, indigenous educational leader, who not only recognizes that Na-tive-based education is crucial to our survival, but who, more importantly, has taken action to evolve new strategies. I give thanks for these leaders ... the warriors, the peacemakers, and the ambassadors. What they share in common is their courage, determination, and passion to make a difference.

Furthermore, I believe this compilation of their collective wisdom about creating meaningful education will make a difference. If this book proves to be an effective way to share the collective wisdom, as we hope that it will, then we believe that generations in the future will benefit. How can we predict that far into the future? We agree with Chief Leon Shenandoah's answer:

> As you walk ahead, look behind you. See your sons and daughters. The future is with us. Look farther, and see your sons' and daughters' children and their children's' children even unto the Seventh Generation. We, in all of our decisions, individually and collectively, are responsible for, and to, the next generations who will be walking the same earthly path we walk today.

Through this book, we hope that we will leave even better paths to education for the generations yet to come.

I am honored that Dr. Maenette Benham asked me to share my thoughts about this work. I have vivid memories of the day the seed for this effort was planted, and am pleased to have been involved as a representative of one of the major funders, the W. K. Kellogg Foundation. When I first learned of the effort, it was only a vision. The initial goal was to gather indigenous education leaders together for a forum focused on sharing knowledge and the best practices for education of Native children from various indigenous groups throughout the world. Dr. Benham worked hard to refine the vision, develop a strategic plan, and submit a proposal. Funding, however, was difficult to secure. In this process, we realized that at the edge of the 21st century, many myths and stereotypes about indigenous peoples persist, and hence, need to be dispelled. We have to provide basic education about Native peoples to professional mainstream educators and philanthropists. Once that hurdle was overcome, it was on to "project implementation and measuring outcomes," or, so we thought.

What followed at Sol y Sombra Ranch in Santa Fe, New Mexico, in July 1997, however, was an incredible gathering that is only partially recounted in this book. No team of individuals could have fully planned the sacred, natural events that occurred, nor could any foundation, even with every resource in the world, have purchased the outcomes. In numerous and magical ways, we were reminded of an attribute that has sustained indigenous peoples for years—a deep sense of spirituality. We thank the Creator for that gentle reminder. *Nyah weh.*

Preface

The purpose of this book is to create a space for the sharing of conversations and for the learning of both truth and wisdom through the ideas of 14 Native educators from around the globe. Their reflections on Native education are contained in the chapters that follow. Here, these remarkable teachers explore ways to enhance and apply a broader, more inclusive body of knowledge that links the "best thinking" (theory and inquiry) on Native education with the "best practices" (leadership, teaching and learning) across diverse, Native communities. What we learn from these leaders is that our thinking and our work must be community based and must facilitate the connection of schools, families, and children as we work across cultures to improve Native education. In addition, we learn that we must fashion a comprehensive curriculum that serves the academic, cultural, spiritual, and physical needs of Native children and youth. Finally, the learning experiences in this curriculum must be rooted in social action, which seeks to transform our current educational system, one that has for so long silenced Native peoples.

This book begins the work of breaking that silence by sharing the voices of Native educators from Australia, New Zealand (Aotearoa), Canada, Alaska, Hawai'i, and from the many Native peoples that stretch from the Atlantic to the Pacific across the 48 contiguous states. We begin, in chapter 1, with a description of our gathering and the vision for a language and cultural-based educational model that arose from that meeting. Throughout the text are Transition sections written by the editors that serve to overview the events of the gathering of Native leaders in the summer of 1997 and that help to link a cluster of chapters to particular themes presented by the *Go to the Source* model. The theme, *Go to the Source*, presented in chapter 1, is essential to the stories that follow because it is framed by both the conversations and the experiences of the participants. The collective vision and wisdom of the *Go to the Source* model for Native education underscores the need for Native educators to remember our indigenous roots and to cling tenaciously to that which has fed us: our language, culture, land, and spiritual past.

Each chapter that follows is written by a Native educational leader and reflects his or her personal model for Native education. Each author has much to teach about locating wisdom that leads to ways of addressing a wide range of social, economic, political, ecological, and cultural issues that Native children and youth confront today. Reflections on this understanding are contained in prologues written by Maenette Benham as well as the short transitional pieces just mentioned. The participant's chapters are clustered around four larger themes that highlight the importance of Native epistemologies, Native language and culture, a connection to spirit and the building of community in the creation of a global indigenous educational model.

We begin this text with a note from the series editor, Joel Spring, Choctaw. In his introduction we can hear the voices of our ancestors and we, in response, begin to extend our spirits to join them in the creation of a more powerful future. Spring's gift of poetry is followed by Valorie Johnson's, Cayuga-Senaca, Foreword. Johnson began our journey by giving thanks to the Creator, then presses us all to create a passage of learning that is responsible, humane, and spiritually sound. The afterword, written by Dr. Beatrice Medicine, our well-respected elder from the Standing Rock Sioux Tribe (North and South Dakota), reminds us to think hard about the ideas posed by the different Native leaders and to ask the essential question, "How can these models be useful in communities of aboriginal peoples and in educational institutions of a dominant culture in which all indigenous peoples of the world interact?"

Compiling this book taught both the editors and the contributors much about deep cultural ways of knowing and the importance of shared power and leadership. Jeannette Armstrong, Okanagon educator, emphasized this learning in her passionate words, "We cannot afford to loose one Native

child!" Indeed, Native peoples, like the individual flowers entwined lovingly into a fragrant lei, must value our interconnectedness and work collectively to assure that our unique histories, languages and traditions are
not lost. This book is an offering to that personal responsibility and commitment each of us has to look within and reach out.

E hoe wa 'a me ka akahele ... paddle your canoe carefully.
Journey well in the breath of life. Aloha.

ACKNOWLEDGMENTS

Mahalo to the courageous educational leaders who have shared their time,
energy, and visions with us. And, to many assistants that have participated
in the many phases of our project: Yvette Luna-Gregory, Rosemary Casey,
Mapula Mahasha, Cathy Robinson, Jeremy Garcia, Ellen Cassidy, Charlie
Baker-Clark, and Robert Benham. A very special thank you to Valorie
Johnson and Rosana Rodriguez of the W. K. Kellogg Foundation, Ingrid
Washinawatok of the Fund of Four Directions, and Robert Floden and
Lynne Frechen of the Institute for Research on Teaching and Learning at
Michigan State University. *Mahalo* to our hosts, the Millers, at Sol y
Sombra, a truly spiritual place. Our special *Aloha* to our editors, Joel Spring
and Naomi Silverman, whose work reveals a deep commitment to Native
issues, social justice and transformation, and indigenous authors.
    As always, we give thanks to our elders who love us on both our good and
bad days, and who never refuse us their wisdom and hope.

—*Maenette Kape 'ahiokalani Padeken Ah Nee-Benham*
—*Joanne Elizabeth Cooper*

'Ekahi (Chapter 1)

Gathering Together to Travel to the Source: A Vision for a Language and Culture-Based Educational Model

Maenette Kape'ahiokalani Padeken Ah Nee-Benham
Joanne Elizabeth Cooper

> Give me back my language and build a house
> Inside it.
> A house of madness.
> A house for the dead who are not dead.
> And the spiral of the sky above it.
> And the sun
> And the moon.
> And the stars to guide us called promise.
>
> —Joy Harjo (*We Must Call a Meeting*, 1990)

THE BEGINNINGS

When we began this work, during the summer of 1996, we knew that it would forever change our lives. Our plan was to bring together a group of respected, Native Hawaiian, American Indian (indigenous people of North America), Alaskan Native, Maori, and Australian Aborigine leaders who championed innovative educational initiatives in their home contexts. We wanted this group to be representative of young-novice and elder-seasoned educators, male and female, from a variety of institutional settings serving preschoolers through adults. The purpose of our work together would be to

1

create a visionary space to talk and to listen, to learn about our uniqueness and similarities, and to share ideas and practices that have supported and shaped learning experiences for Native children and youth. We understood that the ideas that would emerge from the gathering would positively and effectively address many dilemmas confronting Native educators. In particular, we hoped to craft a Native vision, which would replace the English-American model of learning. This model has not only been ineffective, but often destructive to Native ways of knowing and learning. V. Deloria, Jr. (1991/1994) wrote:

> English education, represented first by benevolent members of the aristocracy who gave funds to support Indian schools and later embodied in the United States government's encouragement of mission activities among the frontier tribes, represented, and still represents, an effort to effect a complete transformation of beliefs and behaviors of Indians. Education in the English–American context resembles indoctrination more than it does other forms of teaching because it insists on implanting a particular body of knowledge and a specific view of the world which often does not correspond to the life experiences that people have or might be expected to encounter. (p. 20)

Hence, the hard work of the gathering was to think deeply about how both Native and Western worldviews might coexist in dynamic educational settings that value spirituality and connection to land, language, and ancestry.

We, the Native educators gathered during the summer of 1997, believe that the stories passed on by our *kūpuna* (elders) coupled with our own life experiences and research brought us to this pathway in our individual life journeys. We know first-hand the debilitating affects of Western ideology, assimilation, and cultural genocide on Native peoples of North America, Alaska, Australia, Aotearoa (New Zealand), and Hawai'i. After centuries of indignity, misinformation, and abuse, however, Native pride and activism (fostered by the 1950s–1960s civil rights movement in the United States) has refocused Native peoples attention on self-determination an important action issue. In Hawai'i, for example, the rallying points came from the successful sailing of the *wa'a* (canoe) Hokule'a to Tahiti and the successful struggle for the return of the sacred island of Kaho'olawe (taken by the U.S. military for bombing practice) to the Hawaiian people. These actions have affirmed that Native people must take the initiative to define a course for Native education, which is grounded in our own principles, epistemologies, and cultural values.

On the urging and approval of kūpuna and colleagues, we began the work of this project, In Our Mother's Voice. Many have asked how we came to name this initiative. Maenette explains the naming of our work in a short story that goes like this:

> I believe the name, In Our Mother's Voice, was a special gift from my aumakua (family god) the pueo (owl). One summer day, I was telling my then seven-year-old niece, Lehua, many stories of wā kahiko (ancient Hawai'i). I was surprised that the legends and tales just flowed from a memory space that I had long forgotten existed. Throughout the summer I taught her lessons about the history of the Hawaiian people, how to do things in Hawaiian ways, and important information about the natural environment, the 'āina (land) and the kai (sea), that are the foundation of our island home. I also employed 'ōlelo no'eau, Hawaiian sayings, to teach Lehua Hawaiian values and principles.
>
> This sharing of Hawaiiana through 'ōlelo no'eau, hula (dance) and mele (music), arts and crafts, and storytelling reminded me that the aloha (love and care) passed on from one generation to the next was key to the survival of everything that is Hawaiian. As Native people, what we know about our past and our present comes from the stories that have passed from one body to the next, from mouth to ear, through the voices of our kupuna. Because the power of the word carries truth, cradles emotions, and creates facts, the story can bring to life distinctive ways of knowing. I came to know that the source of all the stories that I had been sharing with Lehua were the voices of my kūpuna past and present. It was their individual and collective voices that evoked the timeless lessons I have learned and now share with Lehua. The message was indeed traveling from one generation to the next, effortlessly, and with so much aloha. I had, without knowing, become the storyteller—the channel if you will—for the voices of kūpuna to the very young.

At the same time that I was teaching Lehua, I was reading Leslie Marmon Silko's book, Ceremony. The opening poem of this story challenges the Native leader to work for social justice.

Ceremony

I will tell you something about stories,
[he said]
They aren't just entertainment.
Don't be fooled.
They are all we have, you see,
all we have to fight off
illness and death.
You don't have anything
if you don't have the stories.
Their evil is mighty
but it can't stand up to our stories.
So they try to destroy the stories
let the stories be confused or forgotten.
They would like that
They would be happy
Because we would be defenseless then.
He rubbed his belly.
I keep them here
[he said]
Here, put your hand on it
See, it is moving.
There is life here
for the people.
And in the belly of this story
the rituals and the ceremony
are still growing.

Becoming both teacher and learner, I came to realize the importance of the stories that our elders have shared. Silko's poem affirms the value of stories in our lives. I think I always knew this, but it became more evident when I had to take on the role and the responsibilities of the storyteller.

For Joanne, the moment she heard the poem's title this importance rang true for her:

Because five generations of the women in my family all carry the middle name Elizabeth, Joanne states: I feel the lineage of these women and their stories in my own life. I come from a family steeped in oral traditions, a family of storytellers who have passed on important ways of knowing and being in the world through their stories. The power of those stories is their ability to carry laughter, love, and wisdom. As a mother of two daughters, I feel a special responsibility to carry the mother's voice from past to present generations.

Stories are the foundation of this book and are shared for different reasons. They are meant to teach, guide, and, in some cases, direct the reader. Some of the stories are everyday ones. We ask that the reader "listen" to the personal stories of pain and struggle in order to connect spirit with spirit to gain deeper meaning. Throughout, there are stories of creation, history, and genealogy that link contemporary people to land or place and ancestry or integrity. Some of the stories are humorous, dramatic, or mystical, but all enlighten us to the importance of linking the mind, body, and spirit to learning and teaching. Finally, sacred stories are shared in the spirit of the book—not written in the text—that reveal respect for ceremony and protocol.

Hence, the purpose of our book and it's title, *In Our Mother's Voice*, is to highlight the importance of the lessons and guidance shared through oral storytelling, of *kūpuna*, both female and male. The feminine voice is chosen for the title only because the woman is the life-giving force and the source of land, rank, political power, and culture, yet both males and females share the responsibility and challenges of perpetuating Native culture and language. Much like the *'ōhi'a lehua* tree that blossoms in even the most rugged, volcanic terrain, the work of this initiative, similar to the work of our *kūpuna*, is to rekindle Native and non-Native passion to *aloha* (love), *mālama pono'ia* (care), and *'ihi* (respect). Additionally, the fruits of this labor must create meaningful, sustainable communities that foster healthy learning environments for it's youth and that are grounded on the principles of *kōkua* (help), *ukupau* (to work together), *'ohana* (family), and *ho'oponopono* (to put right). This has become our passion, *e lei kau, e lei ho'oilo i ke aloha* (love is worn like a wreath through the summers and the winters for the work that lies ahead).

THE PARTICIPANTS AT THE GATHERING

In July 1997 at Sol y Sombra (the last home of artist Georgia O'Keefe) in Santa Fe, New Mexico, we brought together 14 Native educational leaders. The goal of this unique gathering was to provide a forum for educational leaders in which to share, examine, and disseminate Native practices and thinking about learning and teaching in Native settings. Additionally, the information shared would provide tools to assist the preparation of school personnel (e.g., teacher-leaders and school-leaders), to provide information regarding curriculum development and pedagogy, and to respond to questions regarding community partnerships and family involvement.

Joanne and Maenette

Although there was an extensive list of potential participants to draw from, for budgetary reasons we could invite only 14 exemplary leaders. Each brought to the gathering diverse skills and talents, represented innovative programs that sought to revitalize language and culture, and each has been charged with directives that include, but are not limited to (a) defining the areas of need for Native children and youth in their community, (b) developing both a knowledge base and instructional strategies which include the history, culture, art, and language of their Native lineage, and (c) articulating a mission that is deeply Native and that advocates for equity and diversity within a mainstream Western society. We hoped that the scope of their individual work would ensure that valuable contributions would continue to be made to the intellectual, social, instructional, cultural, and ethical development of pre-kindergarten through Grade 16 + Native populations.

Because of the group's diversity, the thoughts they shared through small and large group discussions, model building, as well as individual interviews and journal writing reach across a wide arena of needs and problems. Their contributions were refreshing and beautiful; like the '*ōhi'a lehua* they are bursts of color in a desert of White Western discourse.

A list of the participants follows:

- Sarah Keahi, Native Hawaiian educator
- Sam Suina, Cochiti Pueblo, community college professor
- Genevieve Gollnick, Oneida, curriculum director (K–12)
- Darrell Kipp, Blackfeet, language immersion program
- Jeannette Armstrong, Okanagon, author, researcher, teacher
- Kalena Silva, Native Hawaiian, professor of Hawaiian studies and language
- L.A. Napier, Cherokee Nation of Oklahoma, assistant professor of educational leadership
- Paul Johnson, Ojibwe, educational consultant
- Miranda Wright, Athabaskan, anthropologist and educator
- Susan Wetere-Bryant, Maori, researcher and educational consultant
- Linda Aranga-Low, Maori, K–12 educator
- Kate Cherrington, Maori, educational specialist, Tertiary education
- Gail Kiernan, Australian Aborigine, educational consultant
- Rosalie Medcraft, Australian Aborigine, K–12 educator and author

Additionally, our support team included three graduate students in education. It was our intention to invite students who are committed to working with Native youth, as assistants and co-learners at the gathering. Our hope was that the participants would carry away with them lessons to support their future dreams and good works. Mapula Mahasha, a master's of education student from South Africa, graduated from Michigan State University and is currently a school administrator in her home country. Rosemary Casey is currently a PhD candidate at the University of Hawai'i at Mānoa, and is studying the experiences of Pacific Island students in a Western university setting. Yvette Luna-Gregory graduated with a master's degree in student affairs from Michigan State University and currently works in higher education in an administrative capacity.

Sol y Sombra

THE SETTING: SOL Y SOMBRA

It is important to describe our setting, Sol y Sombra, because it enhanced and deepened our commitments to each other and the purpose of the forum. Our group met in a large lodge decorated in a southwestern style that highlighted the gold, red, and brown colors of the desert. In the center of the large meeting room was a small fountain around which we would gather at the start of each day. We also held our large group discussions around this body of water. Water is significant to many Native groups as it cleanses and brings clarity as well as refreshes and gives life. Above the fountain, in the high, open-beamed ceiling, a large skylight invited streams of sunlight that flooded the room. There were many large sofas and chairs around the perimeter of the room allowing for comfortable, small-group discussions and afforded space for individuals to reflect and write without interruption. Plants and beautiful Native artwork complimented the room, which had large picture windows connecting the interior with the beautiful gardens that surrounded the building.

This environment enhanced our work because it afforded us ample space to create talking and sharing circles. This became both a physical and spiritual necessity as it fostered facilitation of discussion and reminded everyone of the important place circles and ceremony must have in the educational processes. Sylvia O'Meara and Douglas West in their 1996 book, *From Our Eyes: Learning from Indigenous Peoples,* wrote that sharing circles are a "political, social, economic, and historic experience that solidifies the bonds of community" (p. 7). The essence of the circle, which also grounds our *Go To The Source* educational model, is that it advances the concept that social interaction, development of community bonds, and oral traditions are fundamental to indigenous experience and identity.

Sol y Sombra's grounds invited sharing circles and solitude for the Native educational leaders. A midday walk around the property was especially delightful because artful sculptures were placed strategically along the trail among indigenous plants. Benches invited participants to sit and meditate, and at different parts of the trail, absorb the vastness and beauty of Santa Fe and the foothills of the Sangre de Cristo mountains. The property's greenhouse offered a cool and colorful respite on warm afternoons. In the evening, our group shared spectacular sunsets from the rooftop patio of the lodge and relaxed around a wood-burning fireplace.

Following is a poem one participant wrote about Sol y Sombra that poignantly describes the warmth of the locale and expresses its impact on the participants:

Sol y Sombra
by Sarah Keahi

Peace and love are mine
In the lush verdure of Sol y Sombra.
Caressed by gentle breeze,
Kissed by falling rain,
Darkened by peals of thunder,
Energized by streaks of lightning.
Nature enfolds us.
Her beauty abounds.
We hear her heartbeat
'Tis music to our ears.
The scent of pinion permeates the air
We are one in serene tranquillity.

THE GATHERING: ACTIVITIES
AND CONVERSATIONS

The gathering was arranged in three primary segments: *Planting:* Sharing our individual visions for Native education; *Nourishing:* Framing a collective vision for Native Education; and *Harvesting:* Sharing the collective vision—next steps. Each day began with a blessing and ended with concluding thoughts shared by one of the participants. We knew that integrating Native rituals and ceremonies throughout the gathering would increase cross-cultural understanding and dialogue as well as give appropriate respect to the Natives (Pueblo) of the land we were visiting. Our days were filled with discussions that led to understanding differences and similarities about educational history, policy, and practices across Native peoples. There was also much sharing of personal life stories that taught lessons about what Native schooling has and what it ought to look like. Participants moved from frustration to rejuvenation as they grappled with pressing issues and discovered new insights and strategies to improve Native education.

DEFINING A MODEL FOR OUR WORK

In order to define a collective model, we studied the gathering's small- and large-group discussion transcripts, participant's journal writings and interviews, and, in particular, the individual educational models and the collective story. Additionally, using our climb up a mountain to Cochiti Pueblo as a framing metaphor for an educational model helped us see connections across models, translate the messages embedded in the stories, and define important educational principles. Although we felt quite overwhelmed by this responsibility, it was clear that a collective model could not be built on guesswork, but must be grounded on the knowledge and experience of each Native educational leaders at the gathering. Our first observation revealed particular themes that emphasized community building, trust and mutual support, language centered learning and teaching, sovereign leadership, linkages with Native practitioners across the globe, setting Native community goals and action plans, and development of learning experiences that are grounded in Native values and the ancestoral lineage.

Each of the educational models presented in this book accents fundamental commitments to teach Native culture and language, restore memories of the past, and provide vital opportunities for Native youth to embrace their heritage, to learn to negotiate across differences such as diverse paths between the Native and non-Native worlds, and respect collective and individual pathways. Although each participant presented a model that addressed the unique needs of her community, each model is linked to the next in fundamental ways. One may discover universal truths and dreams that are held in common. For example, every educational leader believed that the single most pressing issue facing our Native communities is the question of how to meet the needs of our increasingly diverse student population in a quickly advancing global society. Furthermore, we believe how we address these complicated needs must be grounded pedagogically, epistemologically, and culturally in our unique Native ways of knowing and doing, and within the broader context of school, family, and community.

Given our collective advocacy for building learning communities grounded in Native language and culture, the models presented in this book speak to the need for Native and non-Native school and community leaders to think globally, and work equitably and collectively with elders and families within our communities, to connect internal and external agencies with Native and non-Native experts. We believe networking within and across our communities, can best facilitate change, which will lead to substantive, long-lasting improvements in the quality of learning and living for Native student populations. Every writer, therefore, must call for school leaders to form professional learning communities with leaders and teachers in other tribes across the United States, Canada, Alaska, Hawai'i, Aotearoa, and Australia. These linkages, we believe, afford Native school leaders an opportunity to learn and to share inclusive, innovative, and forward-looking content and pedagogy, infused with equitable and optimal learning experiences.

As we examined each model's uniqueness, we began to see common objectives for Native education. For example, each model promoted intellectually sound curriculum and instruction, that reflects current thinking about learning and teaching. All the educational leaders are deeply committed to the inclusion of Native history, culture, language, and art. Furthermore, they believe that diverse and interdisciplinary learning opportunities should be provided through involvement with the physical environment. Additionally, all participants stressed the importance of building a global community through curriculum, teaching, and environment that fosters self-respect; cultural respect; and productive school, family, and community relationships. The connections that the school has with the community became a key element in cultivating a deep respect for cultural and human diversity. An example of this connection was the inclusion of multiple generations (i.e., elders, parents, siblings) in learning experiences that honor ways of knowing that are grounded in Native epistemologies and beliefs.

Dialogue regarding appropriate pedagogy further brought to the surface principles of teaching and learning that became essential to our understanding of how to restructure Native education. In fact, a book by Dr. Gregory Cajete, a Tewa Indian from Santa Clara Pueblo, played a significant part in several discussions. At one point in Cajete's book, *Look to the Mountain: An Ecology of Indigenous Education* (1994), he explored the ceremony in the teaching and learning of art. Cajete's learning steps capture the essence of our group's discussion regarding the importance of meaning-making and the generation of Native knowledge in the learning and teaching process. Indeed, the features of Cajete's model posit thoughtful ideas for Native educators as they search for and develop new ways of teaching. Here is a synopsis of his steps:

- *Preparing:* This is a conscious effort to simplify, to become aware, to sharpen the sense, to concentrate, to revitalize the whole being.
- *Guiding Spirit:* Consistent adherence to original intent, the idea of applying one's will to concentrate one's whole being into a task.
- *The Sources:* Attention to the nature of the sources of raw materials. Not only the quality of materials was important, but also how and where they were obtained.
- *Adhering to patterns yet transcending them (form or design):* Generally, ceremonial artistry acknowledged the inherent mystery, the intrinsic integrity of both medium and material, but within the parameters and adherence to a sometime strict cultural convention.
- *Time:* A culturally defined dimension; time becomes an artistic and creative ingredient.
- *Right Place:* The place of creation often becomes a consideration. Cajete state that place, environment must be conducive to educational endeavors.
- *Letting Go and Becoming:* Self-effacement and surrender to the contingencies of the task of creation often characterize the production of ceremonial art.

- *Intrinsic Well-Practiced Belief:* It is only appropriate will, sustained by an integrated and properly focused vigil, that will align with an eloquent expression of the truth of a given indigenous group.
- *The Packing of a Symbol:* Indigenous people believe that symbols have a power beyond their literal connotations. ... Each symbol represents a metaphor whose meaning is in the context of the myth, experience, or understanding of a Tribal group or clan.
- *The Vigil:* Sustaining appropriate attention to every aspect of creating an object is not only a reflection of vigilance, but also an honoring of the process of making, through which each detail of work is given its due.
- *The Completion:* In this stage the intent of a created work is crystallized and given physical birth into the human world of use and understanding. As a form, it is packed with potential, but this is not the end of the indigenous artistic process, only a transformation of orientation and focus.
- *The Give Away:* Is where the completed form, and the life and meaning inherent in its physical being, is given up to the purpose and process for which it has been created.
- *Aesthetics and Appreciation of Intrinsic Meaning:* The aesthetics and value of the artifact are directly related to what it means and the purpose it serves in a Tribal context. (pp. 155–158)

In light of these principles, many of the participants shared new ways of governing and organizing their educational settings. For example, many suggested that new organizational frameworks, that facilitate shared leadership and a collective approach toward governance of formal school life, be developed by each community. Some of the educational leaders argued that school communities, in order to remain viable and linked to Native values, must work to support honest and respectful dialogue among all school-related stakeholders (i.e., student, parent, and special interest groups, teachers, policymaking bodies). Members of the gathering agreed that conflict between traditional and contemporary ideas was inevitable, and in many cases healthy, but that conflict negotiation and decision making should be grounded on Native practices such as *ho'oponopono, kiva, sharing circle,* and *talking circle,* to name a few.

Each voice in this book is deeply spiritual, each thought brilliant, each model both visionary and concrete. All believe both the Native and non-Native community must collectively work to assure that Native children become the beneficiaries rather than the victims of schools. Black Elk spoke of this unity:

> Then I was standing on the highest mountain of them all, and round about beneath me was the whole hoop of the world. And while I stood there I say more than I can tell and I understood more than I say; for I was seeing in a sacred manner the shapes of all things in the spirit, and the shape of all shapes as they must live together like one being. And I saw that the sacred hoop of my people was one of many hoops that made one circle, wide as daylight and as starlight, and in the center grew one mighty tree to shelter all the children of one mother and one father. And I saw that it was holy. (p. 43)

The message of this passage provides a dynamic metaphor, that symbolizes the importance of our participation as individuals in a universal and collaborative effort. Our many discussions throughout the gathering were grounded in the belief that it is only through collective work that the many educational problems we currently face can be addressed, problems such as underachievement through inappropriate educational systems, lack of teaching skills, negative peer pressure, low parent aspirations and expectations, and narrow assessment techniques.

Our work to frame a collective model from the diverse and localized models presented by the participants was a tremendous task. We knew that we must honor the lessons learned from each and, at the same time, capture a collaborative vision that might encourage dynamic, fluid interpretations of its principles at the local site. We began by asking two questions: "What is it that we want for our Native children and youth?" and "In light of this, what ought to be the goals for Native education?" We reviewed the models, discussion transcripts, and journals over and over again and found that what we wanted for our Native children was to provide them with the opportunity to grow up surrounded by hearing and speaking their mother tongue. We wanted our children to articulate a Native self-identity, be centered in their unique Native ways of knowing, and live as a proud Native people. Pride and knowledge of one's culture, history, and language meant our children would respect their ancestors and take care of their homeland. Finally, we wanted our children to negotiate confidently the boundaries between their Native and non-Native worlds and make choices that maintained self and cultural integrity.

We continued to explore the shared models, pouring over the words, asking elders for guidance, praying, laughing, crying, and healing while moving forward and inward. Eventually, particular goals for Native education emerged. First, that all-Native educational programs must emphasize Native language development in both written and oral skills and press toward multilingualism. Participants at the gathering believed that holding onto our Native languages, which link us to rich histories and heroic ancestors, was essential, but the reality of living in a global community meant that knowing other languages and histories was equally important. Second, all Native education programs must stress Native understanding of culture and history, past and present, and focus on ways to address current issues. This goal resulted from our experiences with curricular materials that excluded or stereotyped the stories of our Native communities. In essence, historical retelling from a Native perspective was needed and that this movement was an intrinsic piece of building civic and community responsibility.

Our third goal advocates for a curriculum, that is grounded in self-determination, cultural self-esteem, and personal vision and passion. Like our second goal, the genesis of this theme came from our own stories and experiences in educational institutions that marginalized the issues and concerns Native children and youth brought to the classroom. Above all, we believed that learning and teaching must be liberating. In light of this, our fourth goal centers on teaching and learning as processes which build responsibility to self, family, and community while actively involving the extended family and Native community in the learning process. A lesson we all learned in our individual educational journeys and in conversation with one another during the gathering was the necessity to share, encourage, and learn from one another. We learned that isolation results in an idea's speedy death, but that the exchange of ideas and mentoring among Native peoples leads to strength. The fifth goal requires the development and promotion of Native programs and best practices that will significantly improve academic achievement, reduce absenteeism and drop outs, and eliminate social problems among Native children and youth.

Once we were clear about what we wanted for our Native children and youth, and what the goals for a Native education model would be, a more difficult question arose. Because everyone held tightly to the belief that a Native model for dynamic and empowering education must be grounded in Native principles and values, what principles and whose values would we use? We were fearful that any overarching model might smack of *pan-Native* features that ignore the distinctiveness of each particular group. Each participant shared their own views on this question and many reflected on this query in their journals. Reviewing interview transcripts and journal writings, we recognized that whereas the educational leaders cautioned against following only one Native model, Native thought education could be grounded on four principles, which are:

1. Native spiritual wisdom which is guided by the hearts of our grandmothers and grandfathers.
2. Critical development of the intellect which intersects Native ways of seeing and doing with modern ways of seeing and doing.
3. Promotion of a healthy body and healthy environment.
4. Preservation and revitalization of Native languages, arts, and traditions.

Grounded on these four principles, the collective vision took shape as a ring of fire with the sun at its core. We called this vision, *Go to the Source*.

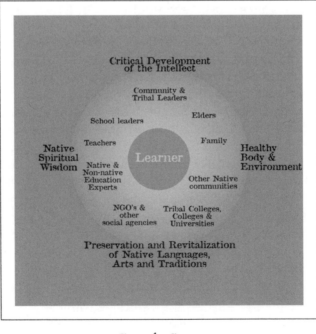

Go to the Source

At the core of this model is the student-learner who connects us to both our past and our future. Indeed, all decisions regarding policy, practice, pedagogy, governance, and organizational structure must support the learner and be grounded on four essential life elements: critical development of the intellect, healthy body and environment, preservation of language, and spiritual wisdom. Because we honor Native ceremony, we must also remember that the four principles must also work collectively to achieve balance at the personal, institutional, and community levels.

These principles illuminate dynamic dimensions of *knowledge, community,* and *family.* Knowledge is key to Native understanding because of the belief that knowledge comes from the ancestors, is passed to us today, and moves forward to the future. This idea challenges a Native person to trust both the lessons learned from the past and to realize, or come to know, the new shapes of knowledge today. The evolution requires a person to transcend finite (factual) knowing and enter into a more abstract, multiple layering of meaning. Deloria, Jr. (1991/1994) wrote: "Traditional knowledge enables us to see our place and our responsibility within the movement of history" (p. 23). The gathering's participants suggested that ones Native language lead to understanding positionality and context because it carries the double entendre meanings of the past and is filled with metaphor, which helps define our present.

Knowledge, then, becomes the responsibility of the community. Deloria, Jr. (1991/1994) wrote:

> Education in the traditional setting occurs by example and not as a process of indoctrination. That is to say, elders are the best living examples of what the end product of education and life experiences should be. We sometimes forget that life is exceedingly hard and that no one accomplishes everything they could possibly do or even many of the things they intended to do. (p. 23)

Hence, this model advocates for community involvement and responsibility in the teaching and learning processes. Our conversations about community brought a striking point to the surface that community is not a birthright. Participants argued that community could only thrive if we believe we belong and we actively participate as members. Deloria, Jr. wrote:

> The old ways of educating affirmed the basic principle that human personality was derived from accepting the responsibility to be a contributing member of a society. Kinship and clan were built upon the idea that individuals owed each other certain kinds of behaviors and that if each individual performed his or her task properly, society as a whole would function. (p. 21)

Therefore, educational endeavors must be interdisciplinary, intercultural, and involve multiple generations from the community. Furthermore, the survival of an educational initiative would also require the involvement of elders, diverse internal and external Native and non-Native agencies, the support of sustained research and development of Native epistemology and pedagogy, and linkages with other Native educational projects. Together, Jeannette Armstrong stated, "the community must wrap all their resources and love around the learner."

Knowledge and community is enhanced by genuine involvement of the family. The 'ohana is the power that tightly weaves this model together into a basket that can carry the generations of the future. The extended family is boundless, as it exists now as in the past, and will continue into eternity by connecting our generations, na pua, na lei, na mamo (our generations past, present, future). Deloria, Jr. (1991/1994) wrote:

> The final ingredient of traditional tribal education is that accomplishments are regarded as the accomplishments of the family and not to the world around us, particularly the people around us, so that we know who we are and have confidence when we do things. (p. 23)

Because of this connection, the family is powerful, for it provides a foundation for a strong sense of spirituality, self, and cultural identity. Our 'ohana, like the kalo (taro), is the core of who we are as Native peoples, and, it is the work of the 'ohana to assure that our nā keiki (children) grow to be strong. I maika'i ke kalo i ka 'oha (The goodness of a taro is judged by the young plant it produces.) To sustain this foundation, all formal educational institutions must frame their decisions and practices to support family empowerment and 'onipa'a, perpetuating our culture through our kūpuna (ancestors).

The circular structure of the model represents, symbolically, the necessity for balance. That is, balanced philosophy and practices that seek inner peace and dignity as well as equal participation and unity; that fosters both oral speaking, listening, and reflection through silence. Our Iroquois cousins, drawing lessons from a medicine wheel, viewed the model as holistic and fostering the believe that community development must occur at multiple levels of the personal, programmatic, and community. For example, on the programmatic level, the model supports strong teacher and leader professional development to increase learning and practice of Native language skills, develop teaching and resource materials that enhance critical thinking and deepens cultural knowing, create dynamic learning experiences in partnership with community and elders, and further understanding of the importance of Native knowing in the teaching process.

In addition, the role of teachers is integral to implementation and the balance of the *Go to the Source Model* (see: Genevieve Gollnick, Sarah Keahi, Darrell Kipp, and Kalena Silva's models). Karen Swisher, in many of her scholarly writings, and her writings with Donna Deyhle, informs us that teachers of Native students have the responsibility to understand and to teach the underlying philosophies and values of their indigenous culture. In essence, teaching that is linked to identity must incorporate oral stories and traditional teaching, teaching environments that honor a connection to nature, the land, and learning that is inclusive of Native worldviews. The participants of our gathering viewed teachers as guides that guide children on their educational journey, and, more importantly, as servants of the community who work to help bring balance to individuals who then in turn create empowered communities. Therefore, on the community level, the *Go to the Source* model urges school administrators and teachers to become proactive community leaders. They then may develop community based activities that integrate traditional and contemporary practices to address pressing social issues; partner with Native and non-Native individuals and groups to create mentoring experiences in academics, skill development, and Native traditions; and increase opportunities for community members to participate in language and cultural events (see Jeannette Armstrong, Genevieve Gollnick, and Paul Johnson's models in this volume).

Darrell Kipp, in his passionate speech to the gathering participants, reaffirmed the importance of the model in this way:

> We cannot dismiss our history of extermination and the removal of our people so that the White man could get to the natural resources. Assimilation through the Indian boarding schools was a large part of this history in which schools were used to acculturate and socialize new values and another way of seeing the world. Today, we see the effects of capitalization, entrepreneurs through gaming. The selling of the Native! Through all of this we see ourselves, our young people and our old people, struggling with the negotiation between the old and the new. So, what occurs in our educational settings is extremely important! Teaching our youth how to maintain the essence and meaning of their heritage through language and cultural practices is important. And, teaching our youth how to negotiate between the traditional and the contemporary is important. Our model is important because it exemplifies a process, a natural process that acknowledges the importance of building relationships within our communities, with our environment, and with

other cultures. So, education, as our model suggests, connects students to "living" in their physical, spiritual and Native environments. This is important.

In essence, our model advocates building strong educational communities that are family centered, preserves and revitalizes Native languages and cultures, and strengthens self-identity and sovereignty. Self-empowerment, in educational settings (i.e., schools), is hard work because it requires sustained efforts on the part of the individual (student, teacher, and school leader) and the community (class, school, and tribal) to reflect honestly on the past and to look critically and pragmatically at the present and the future. *Go to the Source* is a symbol of our journey through visions. Hence, it is a special, collective story that is shared through multiple voices and different experiences, that honors traditional teachings and recognizes and contemplates implications of the present and future. The model reveals our journey to the kiva of the Cochiti Pueblo, the *piko* of the Native Hawaiian, the *longhouse* of the Iroquois, the *dreaming* of the Australian Aborigine, and the *mountain* of the Maori, the source of wisdom, spirituality, and our sacred covenant with nature. It is at this source where we locate the roots of our passion, and where meaning is given to our relationships and to our Native ways of knowing.

ENDNOTES

1. These findings are further detailed in Benham, M. with Heck, R. (1998). *Culture and education policy in Hawai'i: The silencing of Native voices.* Mahwah, NJ: Lawrence Erlbaum Associates.
2. Silko, L. M. (1977). *Ceremony,* p. 2. New York: Penguin.
3. K–16+ signals our recognition that formal educational experiences often reach into community colleges, trade and/or vocational schools, professional development, and higher education (university level).
4. O'Meara, S. & Douglas A. West. (1996). *From our eyes: Learning from indigenous peoples.* Toronto, Canada: Garamond.
5. Diverse is used here to define different career needs of individual students (i.e., technology, scientific, artistic) as well as differences in family context, mixed-ethnicities (i.e., children are both Native Hawaiian and other derived ancestry), home language, and differences in gender, social class, disability, or sexual orientation.
6. Cajete, G. (1994). *Look to the mountain: An ecology of indigenous education,* pp. 155–158. Durango, CO: Kivaki.
7. Neihardt, J. G. (1972). *Black Elk speaks: Being the life story of a holy man of the Oglala Sioux.* Lincoln: University of Nebraska Press.
8. Deloria, V. Jr. (1991/1994). *Indian education in America: 8 essays by Vine Deloria, Jr.* American Indian Science & Engineering Society. Alberquerque, New Mexico.

9. The Hawaiian saying, 'Ōlelo no 'eau, have been borrowed from Mary Kawena Pukui, (1983). *'Ōelo No'eau: Hawaiian proverbs and poetical sayings.* Honolulu, HI: Bishop Museum Press.

10. See Swisher, K. (1990). Cooperative learning and the education of American Indian/Alaskan Native students: A review of the literature and suggestions for implementation. *Journal of American Indian Education, 29*(2), 36–43. Swisher, K. & Deyhle D. (1989, August). The styles of learning are different, but the teaching is just the same: Suggestions for teacher of American Indian youth. *Journal of American Indian Education* (special issue), 1–14. Also see Lipka, J. (1991). Towards a culturally-based pedagogy: A case study of one Yup'ik Eskimo teacher. *Anthropology and Education Quarterly, 23*(3), 203–223.

OUR DIFFERENT PATHS
TO THE SOURCE

Transition I

Path to Native Epistemology: The Lightning Tree

The opening dinner of the gathering began with an Ojibwe blessing and smudging ceremony shared by Paul Johnson. To begin with a Native ceremony paid appropriate respect to the ancestors of the land we were visiting, honored the ancestors of all the Native people gathered, and recognized the importance of each individual's *mana* (spirit, power). Sam Suina, Cochiti Pueblo, wrote this of the opening ceremony:

> Blessings by Paul. Very much needed and good. Blessings and opening prayers at any gathering are good, but especially when indigenous people come together. It creates a sense of spiritual identity and a sense of oneness rooted in the collective good of all life and of the group. Any foundation of education must be rooted in spirituality and in the oneness of all indigenous people.

During our opening ceremonies, Santa Fe experienced a major thunder and rainstorm. Because natural events have significant meaning to most Native groups, the water that was feeding the earth became a spiritual metaphor for our evening activities. Each participant shared detailed stories of their life journey and related current tensions in their work as educational innovators in their communities. As each story unfolded, vivid and explicit, the connections between hearts and souls became visible. And as the power of the storm grew stronger, the bonds that connected each individual member of the group were cast with love and care. Johnson wrote of the experience:

> Group descriptors include the following: impressive, humorous, intelligent, hardworking, and spiritual. I listen to all of their introductions and I see people working and implementing programs for the benefit of Native people. These people have knowledge, but also have the ability to implement their ideas. The group shows a good sense of humor. We seem to be able to laugh at ourselves. I should have known that this would be the case.

A defining moment was when a bolt of lightning hit the second oldest sequoia tree in Santa Fe, splitting it in four directions. That evening, when the rain stopped, our *Cochiti Pueblo* cousin, Sam Suina, honored the lightning-split tree through ceremony. To Sam's people, a tree that had been struck by lightning is a sign of strength and promise. Sam shared with the group that the grandfathers and grandmothers of the land had blessed our work. The next morning, many in our group honored the tree. The tree became a symbol of the work that lay ahead, and a stick from the tree became our *talking stick*. It became an important reminder of our spiritual link to the past and future, to our ancestors, and to the Earth that sustains all people.

Touched by the power of the"lightning tree," we recommitted to the work of learning and teaching. Our first day of discussion centered on the need for Native leaders to define an educational model that is indigenous in origin and illuminates the ontological essences of Native people. Sarah Keahi reminded the group that a Native epistemological framework must "embrace family, health, and spirituality." Sam spoke passionately about how education carries the lessons of ancestors. The theme of calling on Native voices was repeated in Darrell's metaphor:

> Restoration of knowledge to our younger generation can be seen as the metaphor of fingers (pointing to his thumb to index finger to middle finger to ring finger). Knowledge is transferred from great-grandmother, to grandmother, to mother, and to daughter (holding his little finger). The concept of time and timing, time is running out, we are letting things go.

Silence. Darrell's metaphor had moved the group to deep reflection. A member of the group asked, "Why are we letting things go?" In the dialogue that followed, it became evident that because the Native voice has not been recognized as a "legitimate voice in the arena of pedagogy, so, what is true for our people is not included in the larger picture" (Susan Bryant). Darrell,

Kalena, and Genny affirmed Susan's conclusions and added that privileging occurs in the purveyance of knowledge through mainstream methods of teaching and narrowly defined disciplinary content.

Darrell was unwavering as he advocated for Native control of education, commenting that traditional schools had "failed Native people! Indeed we must abandon these institutions." He argued that Native communities must have barriers that protect the Native populace from continued oppression, mainstreaming, and "Western intrusion." He spoke of the need for Native groups to be suspicious of outsiders:

> We have to be selective. We need to be with those who understand what we [Native educators] do. Start with those who really want this type of education [Native language immersion]. Strengthen those who really are working hard. Our task should be to help our children to have choices and to restore our Native languages. Our children should know their language well. Land and language are critical issues to us. We must have a place to go [where our own language is spoken], a home where our children must come home to. It is a place that they identify with. I am suspicious. Big foundations and government have been using Indian land and resources for many years. They are growing, but they give very little back to indigenous people. We must have our home. Home is powerful. Money can provide buildings and tangible things, but time and space is important. We are running out of space as land is taken from us. Time is also running out.

Genny, who agreed with Darrell, spoke of the need to ground schooling and school-related activities in fundamental values and principles that are defined by a group's unique heritage. As an example of the power of this action, Genny related the work at Oneida, which had defined a Native educational model utilizing their turtle metaphor that links them to *Sky Woman* (see chap. 10). As a result of this challenging new framework, the Oneida Turtle School is recognized as a national blue ribbon school.

Jeannette also agreed with Darrell and Genny, adding, "We should have principles in the process of building our model. We should make the Native language a priority. It is language that makes you what you are. Our models should be centered around children and include liberation." Sam added that, "togetherness brings blessings to us for it creates a sense of spiritual identity. Any learning should support the community and should create a strong sense of cultural identity in young people." Finally, both Sarah and Rosalie added the necessity of including elders, as guides and teachers, to the learning process.

This highly charged discussion clearly identified the need for Native leaders to define an epistemology that will emerge from Native ways of thinking in regard to time, space, relationships (as bound to nature), and orality as central to learning and knowing. In addition, a Native framework such as this must counter dominant educational models that have subjugated the Native as an outsider. In an effort to guide the group to define a Native paradigm, we asked each participant to construct a model of his or her vision for Native education. We provided a variety of art supplies that participants could use to build their model. These included blocks, play-doh, paints, construction paper, pipe wire, beads, feathers, popsicle sticks, plastic animals, cars, leaves, flowers, and earth from the gardens. Because we had explained this activity to the participants prior to the gathering, many brought cultural pieces, heirlooms, and educational tools that would enhance their model.

Each educational model developed by the Native educational leaders is presented. Although all the models illuminate the principles of the *Go to the Source* model, each has a particular feature that we have chosen to highlight in this book. The first three models provide a clear Native epistemological basis for education. This replaces a sociocultural and political hegemony, that has previously supported the stratification and maginalization of Native peoples. At the end of Kate's model presentation, she shared her love for education ending with, "We need to see our Native students as joy!" Later, Kalena Silva echoed Kate's words in this journal entry:

> Such a beautiful day! Like flowers opening in the morning sun, participants continue to open up with their innermost hopes, dreams (and fears) for our people. An important theme stressed repeatedly in presentations was the importance of community—the source of any worth of substantial progress to be made in this work. Communities taking control of the knowledge and direction of schools, working closely with professionals to ensure the best language and culture for their children. Another important theme, after a community has set priorities, it needs to go after them no matter how daunting the task.

'Elua (Chapter 2)

Building a Child-Centered Model: *"An indigenous model must look to the future."*

Kate Cherrington
Te Wananga O Aotearoa

Prologue

Kate Cherrington, the youngest participant at our gathering, embodied the vision of the Go to the Source model. Of Maori descent and a Native speaker of Maori, she is deeply rooted in her Native language and culture as well as skillful and capable in a modern society. Currently completing her master's degree in educational administration, Kate is fluent in dual cultures and languages and can span the boundaries between the Native and non-Native world. Kate recently left her responsibilities as education advisor for Te Wananga O Aotearoa, a Maori tertiary training initiative, to raise two children. Her tane (husband) continues to work for the institution as the educational manager. Kate's model for Native education reflects her own life journey as well as a powerful belief that education must place the child nurtured by extended family and community at its center.

Evident in every model is the importance of the child–youth learner and the need for the family to be involved in the holistic development of the child. Because children are gifts from our creator, they must be at the center of love and nurturing from a circle of extended family and community members. Kate's model captures the essence of this ideology and presses Native leaders and educators to develop and provide instruction and guidance that children and youth need in order to be grounded in their Native culture and language and successful in their rapidly changing global world. Another feature of Kate's model, which is repeated in other models, is the need for every child to have an adult mentor; someone who loves, cares, and praises the child.

Kate introduced significant aspects of an educational vision that were repeated in other models. For example, all the models call for a sovereign theme that defines a self-determined people. This requires that Native peoples determine their educational journey through policy development and implementation. Additionally, most of the models acknowledged the tension created by accelerated changes in our modern world. New discoveries, inventions, and the introduction of new ideas and diverse people can leave unique traditions and languages behind. Kate speaks to the need for Native groups to hold fast to Native values while developing dynamic, forward thinking educational strategies and new learning. Finally, Kate encourages the need for models and processes to include Native and non-Native peoples. It is appropriate that we start with Kate's model, because Kate was our gift from the creator to this gathering.

Kate's daughter, Tuakoi.

Kate Cherrington and her child-centered model.

The center of the model represents life and learning. The shape symbolizes the *whenua* (womb). The child is at the bottom and the mother is at the top. This shape could also be viewed as the *tuakana–teina* (older–younger sibling) or the *mokopuna–tupuna* (grandchild–grandparent). All related to the concept of *kaiako–akonga* (student–teacher). I believe it is very important that in the center of the education model there is a child, a student, and a learner. It is from this center that the meaning and reason for education originates. The mission and the framework on which to build an indigenous model of education comes from this center. The most important focus of this model is the middle, the child, or, learner.

Represented around the student, the child, and the learner is a triangle. Each of the three sides is a different colour. On one side, the colour black represents *te hinengaro*, the intellect, or, the mind. The colour green represents *wairua*, the spirit. The bottom line is the colour red to represent *te tinana*, the body. These three elements form the holistic approach to education and curriculum. Surrounding the triangle and learner are the physical elements that define our world. On the right top side, I've put *te whenua*, the Earth, or, land. A fern frond, the female element, represents life and learning. On the left is the *te rangi*, the sky, weather, and winds. This represents the ever changing nature of education. On the bottom is *te moana*, the sea.

I placed the sea here because a colleague, Janice Eketone, created a wave model that represents organizational structure and development. In brief, as a structure develops and strengthens there comes a point in the wave where it curls in and looks back on itself. This does not mean that the structure has stopped, failed, or declined; it represents a time of reflection, drawing together to evaluate and assess before moving forward. Each wave in the model represents core structural values needed to successfully manifest the ideals and philosophy of the indigenous model. In the wave is written the words *tino rangatiratanga*. This can mean self-determination or sovereignty in a number of contexts. In this instance, *tino rangatiratanga* represents the need for indigenous people to begin the mission, the *kaupapa* (philosophy), of their work within their own cultural value systems. This is paramount in setting the direction for the implementation of a global indigenous vision for education. Therefore, leadership, curriculum, community, facilitation, money, and advocacy each have a place in this wave structure. We cannot ignore the importance of financing, coupled with advocacy of non-Native peoples, as a vehicle to meet the aspirations and goals set by this model.

I believe this value comes from my *tupuna* (ancestors). Our subtribe is *Ngati Hine*, named after our *tupuna Hineamaru*. Hineamaru epitomizes for us *mana wahine*. She bore a child underneath her armpit and was hospitable to strangers, taking them into her home at a time when this was not the custom. From her we learn the lesson, "*Manaaki te tangata, ahakoa ko wai, ahakoa no hea.*" That is, look after people no matter who they are and no matter where they are from.

The spiral and *poutama* (stairway to heaven) represent that our holistic model is a developing, growing, dynamic, not static, model. An indigenous model does not mean all our teachings are based in past, pre-Colonial context, but that the model must also look to the future. I want to emphasize the importance of learning in this model. This block, which is blue, represents business and technology. Native people must grasp the tools of the present and the future. We must teach our children how to use these tools as vehicles through which to manifest Native aspirations. Technology and business systems are important to tools understand because the can help us to fulfill different purposes.

The beads represent people. The beads are of different colours because I believe strongly that this indigenous model must be inclusive, not exclusive. It is not just for Native people, but also for non-Natives. The organization I worked for, Te Wananaga O Aotearoa, is an organization with a mission to educate all peoples through a strong *kaupapa* Maori and within a student-centered foundation. I have plaited the three colours of the triangle together to represent that our approach to learning and to delivery is holistic and connected to learning styles, that are student-centered. We have a student- or learner-centered approach to the delivery of the curriculum; therefore, we recognize the student as a whole person.

Family is important in this model. I was born as the *kauae mua*, or the *mataamua* (the first born), and was privileged to have parents who invested energy and love in me. One of the most important things my father taught was to listen. I believe that lesson has impacted the way that I learn. I observe and experience life. My father also has strong beliefs on the role of women in society. He believed that my mother should not carry sole responsibility for the everyday aspects of raising children. He worked to raise all of his daughters. He claimed that a man must love a woman ten times more than a woman loves a man. My mother is *Pakeha* (non-Native), born to a strong, middle-upper-class family from the South Island, in Bluff. On meeting my father and becoming engaged, my mother came up against many prejudices within her family and blatant racism from the community. My mother fought hard for her children, for equity, and became a resource teacher of Maori in the 1970s. A teacher, my mother had strong opinions on the importance of education and fought hard for girls and women in the educational system. At times, my mother's journey has been lonely and difficult. I acknowledge her in this writing.

Next, I provide an example that reflects the model that has just been described. The stories that I have to share relate to the celebration of the learner as an individual and as a member of *whanau* (family) and community. My children, Tuakoi and Tahuaroa, attend a special early childhood center, Te Amokura Kohanga Reo (Amokura language nest). This is a community based program, in an urban setting, where children and their *whanau* (family) from many tribes, races and ethnic affiliations attend. This *kohanga reo* provides a culturally supportive Maori learning environment for the whole family and their community. The name *Amokura*, given by an elder, Raiha Sergeant, has significant meaning. The Amokura bird's rich red feathers are highly prized and treasured by Maori. Because the Amokura bird also carries and spreads the seed of *Tane*, the guardian of the forest and birds, it symbolizes new life and survival. The seeds represent our treasured children. Our children are the vessels that carry the Maori language and culture into the future and ensure the survival of new generations of human beings who identify as *Tangata Whenua*, the indigenous peoples of Aotearoa New Zealand.

Te Amokura Kohanga Reo focuses on the child, family, and the important principle of *tino rangatiratanga*, Maori self-determination and advancement. This is a founding principle of *kohanga reo* and a fundamental canon of the Treaty of Waitangi. The aim of the *kohanga reo*, therefore, is to develop and strengthen the *mana* of *tino rangatiratanga* and all things that reflect Maori values and belief systems. The *kohanga reo*, as an early-childhood site of learning, provides children and their families with the means to strengthen and pass on their knowledge of language and culture in appropriate Maori ways. All instructional materials are in the Maori language and many cultural stories and songs are integrated in the content of the learning experience. This process ensures that Native knowledge will not be lost in a state (government) system that is founded on assimilation policies and practices.

The principles and values of Maori *tino rangatiratanga* are also reflected in numerous ways through daily practices at Te Amokura Kohanga Reo. For example, all conversation and instruction is in the Maori language. This is a total language immersion "nest" where Native language is valued and practiced. Additionally, our values are revealed through ceremony. Each day begins and ends in prayer. The first activity of the morning begins with a child standing to deliver a greeting that describes their tribal affiliation, the canoes that carried their ancestors to Aotearoa, and the names of the mountains, rivers, seas, tribal meeting grounds, and *marae* (houses) that their tribe identifies with. This allows children to discover and connect to one another, to their ancestors, and to the environment. This way of learning truly embraces the child, the family, and the community in a culturally appropriate way. It is a privilege to have this opportunity so my own children may experience this family based, indigenous education program.

'Ekolu (Chapter 3)

A Holistic Education, Teachings From the Dance House: "We cannot afford to lose one Native child."

Jeannette Armstrong
En'owkin International School of Writing

Prologue

The breadth and depth of a holistic model was developed further by Okanagan scholar, Jeannette Armstrong's vision for Native education. Kate identified the elements of learning as te hinengaro (intellect), wairua (spirit), and te tinana (body). Jeannette added a fourth level, the need for emotional development. She then introduced the dimensions of depth and breadth to our understanding of Native epistemology. Jeannette explained that the intellect, spirit, emotion, and body must also be developed at four levels, which include self, family, community, and land. This, Jeannette teaches, brings together all the aspects of human life.

Underlying Jeannette's model is her understanding that Native children and youth are drawn to pop culture and away from the traditions of their Native people. In light of this, her efforts have focused on teaching Native language and values while connecting the child to cultural self-esteem, to the healing power of family, and to the responsibility of building community and the preservation of Native lands. To do this, Armstrong looks for ways to include a variety of institutions, Native and non-Native, in the learning process, as well as diverse teaching styles and methods that incorporate Native and non-Native ways. For example,

35

her work has challenged Native youth to produce film documentaries on land and water rights, currently volatile issues in their community.

Jeannette's teaching calls for political action to recover and revitalize Native language and culture. This voice to reclaim language, history, and education is heard in every model included in this text. The passion of each Native leader is to seek official recognition of their Native language, to create policy that integrates Native language into schooling and governance, and to develop Native-based teacher education, leadership, and curriculum and instruction. This, as Jeannette advocates through her model, is the pathway to saving our Native children and youth.

Jeannette Armstrong

JEANNETTE'S MODEL FOR EDUCATION

There are four concentric circles that surround the centerpiece I call the *Dance House*. Each circle corresponds to an important element; first, there's the self, then the family, followed by the community, and all brought together by the land. You can also see four quadrants that, in the Okanagan traditional sense, form the whole person. These fundamental areas are the

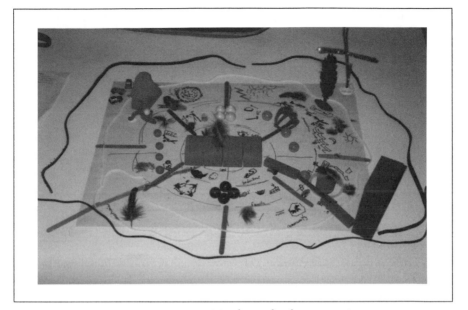

Jeannette Armstrong's *Teachings for the Dance House.*

physical self, the intellect, the spiritual, and emotional. Also, notice that the four quadrants fall in each of the concentric circles. So, one quadrant contains self, family, community, and land.

Let's take one quadrant, the physical self—the "me" underneath my skin. The first concentric circle, "self", says that I must do everything I have to do to keep my physical health. I need to exercise and get the best nutrition to be well. In terms of education, if I am well I have the best chance of being accomplished at anything. Wellness impacts my learning. If I do not get the proper nutrition or exercise there might be problems with me being able to do a number of things. While the first fundamental area of learning, from the physical quadrant, is physical health and well being, physical self also means the physical health of my family members. This is the second circle of family. We are referring to how we are physically connected to our family in terms of what we do together, so that we are all contributing members of the family. All the teaching of sexuality, hormonal processes that take place as we age, and becoming parents and elders need to be taught within the family. We learn relational skills from our experiences with our family. Family physical health is extremely important.

This understanding of how to work, how to contribute physically to one's family, is an important lesson that must be learned in order to be able to contribute to community—our third circle. We are talking about participating physically in ceremony, the work of the community, and in the growth and caretakership of the community. It also means the protection of the land on which your community is based. All of this is built on a strong foundation of physical self and family. It is at the community level that we interface with the land. We need to understand that the relationship between the community and the land constructs how the community behaves, how it operates, what decisions it makes. In a physical sense, what the community does severely impacts the land in a healthy or an unhealthy way. It is also at this level that we touch other groups that surround us, and how together, we become responsible for our environment. You can say that the stewardship of our environment grows out of how well we treat our own bodies.

The fourth quadrant is the emotional one. What we refer to is like we have physical health we also need emotional well-being. The first circle tells us that we have to have a real fundamental love for ourselves and for all the things with which we have been gifted. We need to feel good about ourselves. We must feel that we are capable and self-affirmed. Most important, we have to feel that we have the right to *be*. A right to be *alive!* A right to be what the Creator wants us to be. So in this circle we have all those ideas of identity and affirmation, self-worth, and self-value. This self must be our foundation.

With a healthy affirmation of self we can move to the second circle of family—the relationships with family members. Observe family intimacy that is impaired or dysfunctional and you can really see the importance of a strong self-foundation. If the self is healthy, relationships with family members have a greater chance of being healthy, too. Family is important to education. If a family is healthy learning has a better chance of thriving. We need to understand that the emotional health of our families has a big impact on our children and the generations of children that follow. This is where the biggest breakdown in learning occurred for Native people. The separation of children from their parents and families to attend residential schools created dysfunction. Children didn't know how to build healthy relationships. What has to happen is education must find ways to re-establish family connections to learning and reconnect the child to who he or she is as a Native person.

Next is the concentric circle of community. Two questions arise: How do family and other individuals, in a functional and healthy way, contribute, celebrate, and work together? What governance and social rules does the community enforce? For each community, nation, or tribe there will be a different response and different ways of governance, but we need to understand that the emotional health of the self and of the family is tied to the healthy relationships of the community. And a healthy community is tied to functional families and others who feel a sense of belonging. For example, individual people are feeling alienated today, and this alienation is undermining families and communities. When people and families feel alienated in a community they disassociate themselves from participating in positive relationships and they do not participate in community building. Disassociation is evident in the psychosis behind shootings, killings, and all types of violence and abuse.

Alienation can come when people have to actually disengage from family because they are going to live in a world in which mobilization for jobs and career require them to disconnect or move away from family. In other words, if you come from a Native community and you have to live in New York you would have to disengage emotionally from family, extended family, and community. In traditional Native teachings, one of the things that is said is that when a person does not have community, they do not have family and part of their whole self is emotionally missing. In our teaching, if you do not have family and community, it is almost like you are operating without hands and arms. I think most of us, because we need community and family, will try to recreate community and family wherever we are. There is a great need to be healthy and whole. I believe education must provide opportunities to build emotional health of the self, family, and the community.

We next go to the intellectual quadrant. This is our capacity to analyze, to hold, and to implement knowledge, and to make choices and decisions. We need to understand that our intellect is hooked to our physical self. In other words, you cannot make good decisions if you are hungry or unhealthy. Intellect is also tied to emotional self because you cannot make good decisions if you are abused and all you have is anger or grief. When there is a lot of emotional and physical trauma in your life, you are at a disadvantage because your decisions will not be based on a healthy self. So, when I talk about intellect, I am not referring to how well you think is dependent solely on how well you can objectively analyze or logically process something, but that intellectual ability is a matter of how well your analytical processes are supported by the emotional and physical health of the self. When you are healthy, then the decisions you make and how you "process" the world is based on a whole understanding.

In an educational context, we need to relate the skills we learn in school, whether they are academic or nonacademic, to each of the circles. We need to ask these questions: "How does this learning objective help students develop self?", "How does this curriculum help students to build better family relationships?", and "How does this academic subject help students to become contributing members of the community?", "How does this course of learning help students be better stewards of the land?" "How does this information in economics and the humanities relate to self, family, community, the land, and the world?" If we were to construct our educational plan around questions like these, schools would look very different.

Regarding the fourth quadrant, closest to my intended meaning is the spiritual dimension. This does not have organized religious connotations that implies dogma. The way that we understand spirituality, in the Okanagan sense, is that everything, including ourselves, is part of everything else. We are a part of the land, a part of the community, a part of the family, and so on. We do not have any clear way of understanding this except when we let ourselves become involved in celebration. I guess celebration is the most accurate word. It is the celebration or the connection, with creation that gives us insight to understanding how we are connected to family, community, the land, and so on.

It is within this quadrant that we locate our understanding of ceremonies, songs, and the arts. All of the huge and wonderful things that we see around us, our land and our people, cannot really be appreciated if we do not build cultural context through the ceremonies. For instance, through our ceremonies, we can look at a tree and we understand how we are spiritually connected to that tree. We know that through ceremony and the original teachings we can come to understand our own spirituality, or, you can call it your philosophy, of the world. If we look at the world through the eyes of generations past, to the time when ceremonies were constructed, we can begin to see how each ceremony helps us to sustain, maintain, and pass on those philosophical values that affirm family, community, and land.

Through all the quadrants of this model, the physical, the emotional, and the intellectual, we practice our spirituality. It brings the model together and it expresses our value system at the family, community, and universal levels. An educational process must help the individual to see what is valued most and what we celebrate most, and to be able to see it at the Creator's level. This is what is missing from education. In fact, this spirituality has been critically subverted and taken out of the educational process as though it had no place. It is only all right on Sundays or "special occasions" as the case may be. Yet, spirituality, should be understood, embraced, and practiced daily.

The spirituality of our dances, songs, feasts, festivals, and ceremonies celebrate the self, the family, the community, and the land. The spirituality of our ceremonies is about renewal and regeneration. We continuously celebrate because it is a reminder of our constant enjoyment of self, family, community, and land. It is almost like sinking below the surface to see the connections of all things and being affirmed through this sight. We hold giveaways, and potlatches only after the affirmation that we are healthy physically, emotionally, and intellectually. In other words, you cannot be spiritual if you are not being spiritual at the physical level, at the emotional level, and at the intellectual level. You cannot be abusive to your body or to your family or to your community in any of those ways and still claim to be spiritual. That is how our people see it in the Dance House. So your spirituality and your depth of spirituality is dependent on the things that you have done and the growth and the learning that takes place in each of the other quadrants (physical, emotional, intellectual).

Our educational construct needs to consider where the gaps are and where the breakdowns are in the model between the quadrants and the concentric circles. We need to understand what caused those breakdowns so that education becomes a process to liberate people from a construct that sustains ill health and unwellness. Education moves the construct to sustain good health and well-being, breaks down and replaces dysfunction with better practices that are more encompassing of family and community. We are not looking for someone who can be a math whiz or someone who can be a long distance runner and win a gold medal. What we are looking for in an educational model is for each person to have the chance to learn and understand, to build on the information, and be able to extend that knowledge to their own family to as many others as possible within their community.

We need to look at how communities and families can "plug into" the process and into educational systems. What we are talking about is that the Dance House, in the center, is not a real physical structure, but is symbolic of a process. This process is able to see the whole construct (model) and may find ways to develop strategies to address educational needs. All four quadrants depend on one another, they are interrelated and there are four concentric circles moving outward that are interdependent as well. So, there is no one that does not come from a family or community or land base.

This process I mention is one by which Native, indigenous people make decisions and one process with which our people govern not only them-

selves and their families but their community as well. The word for this process comes from our high language of the Okanagan. The medicine people
and chiefs use it. The word itself describes a process that I think is an important aspect of this model in terms of how it works. For example, if we had a
problem rise up in which we had to make a decision, we would engage in the
process. Usually, the chief or someone who expected to have had learning
in all of the quadrants takes charge of running this process. They may say:

> We don't really understand what this problem is about, but there's lack of un-
> derstanding. One side understands this and another side understands that.
> And what's happening in this conflict is somebody is trying to get the other
> side to agree to their side. Rather than spend our time trying to argue, lobby,
> or politicize each other, what we'd better do is outline for each other what
> our view is. We hear each other out.

What I want to convey of this process, is that there is a good reason why I
would need to understand what you have to say because we have got to get
along here, we are in a community or a family together. We cannot afford to
have this disagreement between us. We have got to hear each other out, so
we can come to a good solution, and then we will be in harmony again. So,
in a community, in a family, or in a work place this process is extremely necessary. The founding principle is one where you concentrate on how to create, at the very foundation, a process of communication to bring about
understanding, to decrease polarities, and to create a balance. You are trying to create balance rather than increasing conflict and confrontation. We
have imbalance, and serious conflicts on many reservation communities between the traditionalists and the progressives, the young and the elders, and
the "networkers" and the "doers."

If we were thinking about public education for the non-Native as soon as
we talk about family, community, and land base it all breaks down because
of the diaspora of generations of people away from a land base. Also, because of the way this market economy is constructed, it takes people from
job to job and away from each other. They have to survive. Community becomes something else other than what an indigenous community is. And
yet, that is where, at the community level, the irresponsibility toward land
and toward social justice occurs. It becomes very important that we look at
a model in which we reinstate strong family, strong community, strong values, and actually talk about reinstating spirituality within all of that. The
strength, I think educationally, is what's going to change the world.

We, as a family group, decided to call the center of education in our extended family the *Dance House*. In this way, learning is always tied to the spiritual and emotional well-being of our family members, that is also tied to the Dance House and its celebration of life. We decided to undertake this because it has not happened in the public school and it is slow to happen on our reservation. Gradually, we are seeing the outcomes in the En'owkin center and in our spiritual educational camp and band schools. More and more children from the entire community are participating. An outcome has been that we now have cultural Okanagan life ways (values) in our schools that call on our extended family members to participate in the cultural and language learning.

We (family) made the commitment to work with our Dance House as our center using our traditional practices, celebrations, feasts, language, and customs. We decided to practice this educational model for our community to help replace the dysfunction that residential schooling had caused, but to do it in a nonconfrontational way. We have not gone and said, "You've got to change your educational system!" We have simply started our own educational plan and process and have carried it out. We now have ten teachers in our family that have been certified by the province. These teachers are also certified by our people as instructors–mentors in medicine, language, and traditional cultural practices. They are the most sought after people in our Indian schools, and even now, the public school is reaching out to borrow them.

It has taken since the mid-1980s to get the extended family to solidify their own learning to set the groundwork for this change, but it has been a really powerful process. What impact it will have 20 years from now! We can just guess. We are seeing the beginnings now. Language revival and spiritual practices of the Okanagan since the mid 1990s have swept our community. Our children and youth are becoming stronger and are growing up with the principles of always being connected to wellness in their family, their community, and on the land. They are participating in it (using learned principles) and are comfortable and natural with it. We are going to have good leaders when they come into full maturity.

'Ehā (Chapter 4)

Grounding Vision on the Three Baskets of Knowledge:
"Kia ora ai te iwi Maori."

Linda Aranga-Low
Maori Educator

Prologue

A significant goal of the Go to the Source model, the integral link between very diverse groups, is a call to action to reclaim Native languages and Native rights to determine the shape and content of Native education. To summarize, Native language-based educational initiatives took shape during the 1970s in New Zealand among the Maori iwi (tribes). The movement began with the Kohanga Reo (1982). This "language nest" program, developed for the early childhood setting (ages 6 months to 6 years), was a total Native language and culture immersion program that brought the entire family and community into the learning process.

This movement for revitalization and preservation of Native language and culture through schooling was soon joined by Native Hawaiian groups in Hawai'i through their Pūnana Leo initiative. The model of language immersion in early childhood education was brought to the North American continent through several initiatives, in particular, the highly respected work of the Piegan Institute on the Blackfoot reservation. The Kohanga Reo, the flagship for language revitalization, was a significant movement because it was championed by Native community elders. This grassroots effort pressed for government policies which soon saw the birth of the Kura Kaupapa Maori, K–12 schools that were taught in the Maori language with Maori philosophies and pedagogies. Over time, this has led to other bilingual programs and the recognition of Maori language, culture, and protocol in mainstream schools.

The political action to officially recognize Native language and to incorporate it in the language of governance and education has resulted in policies that have created K–12 language immersion schools in New Zealand and Hawai'i. Linda's model presents the historical journey of this movement that has challenged all Native educational leaders and persuasively reminds us to ground our models on the principles of our own cultural lineage. In addition, Linda reminds Native educational leaders that because there are many Native children in non-Native educational settings, we must work hard to assure that mainstream schooling is not absent of Native history, language, and culture.

Linda, with her brother, Mike (l) , and her husband, Graeme (r).

LINDA'S INTRODUCTION

Hutia te rito o te harakeke
Kei hea te komako e ko?
Maku e kii atu
He aha te mea nui o te Ao?
Ka kii mai koe ki ahau
He tangata he tangata he tangata.
Te whare e tu nei

Te marae e takoto nei
Tena korua
Nga hau e wha
Nga iwi e tau nei
Tena koutou tena koutou tena koutou katoa
Ko Maungapohatu te maunga
Ko Wai Karemoana te moana
Ko Mataatua te waka
Ko Tuhoe te iwi
Ko Ngati Manunui te hapuu
Ko Linda Aranga-Low ahau
No Aotearoa

My introduction is a traditional format for paying respect to the gathering, the structures within which we are gathered, and introducing myself by describing the important aspects of my geographical and genealogical origins. In this way, I offer my humble contributions.

Maori are the indigenous people, or *tangata whenua*, of New Zealand. The Maori are a colonized and oppressed people—strangers in their own land. One of the major institutions instrumental in causing and continuing this situation was, and still is, the education system. Maori knowledge was reduced in status to that of witchcraft and superstition, and children were beaten for speaking

Linda's grounding vision on the *Three Baskets of Knowledge*.

their language at school. In the 1970s, many Maori could see and feel the terrible damage done to their culture and were greatly afraid of losing their language completely. So they set on a path to revival and survival. In order to set a solid foundation for this, they looked back into ancient Maori knowledge. In Maori mythology, Tane was one of the children of *Rangi* the sky father and *Paptuanuku* the earth mother. Tane's task was to ascend through the levels of heaven to retrieve knowledge and wisdom for his people. On achieving the highest level, he was met by the supreme being and given three baskets of knowledge. These *kete*, or baskets, represent the three divisions of knowledge, and can be viewed as a curriculum for all time.

The first is the *kete-uruuru-matua*, the basket of peace, goodness, and love. My personal symbol of this is a photo of my family in our ancestral home.

The second is the *kete-uruuru-rangi*, the basket containing prayers, incantations and ritual. I have chosen elements of nature to include a bottle of water, green foliage, and a potato—all symbols with specific ritualistic importance.

The third is the *kete-uruuru-tau*, containing knowledge of peaceful arts that promote the welfare of mankind and of war. For this I chose this small example of *raranga*, or *weaving*, and this a *pounamu*, or *greenstone*, shaped as a *patu*, or, war club.

This knowledge then, formed the basis for the *kohanga reo*, or language nests, that provided pre-school babies and infants five day a week care and total immersion in Maori language at all times. This was within a structure based on Maori spiritual values, concepts, and knowledge. The rapid success of *kohanga reo* released hundreds of Maori 5-year-olds with a knowledge of spoken Maori, customs, and values into an educational system lacking in the most basic support structures. In order not to lose the confidence and hope engendered by the success of kohanga reo, parents and communities demanded an extension of the structure into primary schooling (ages 5–11). In 1985, the first *kura kaupapa* Maori, full-immersion Maori elementary school, began at Hoani Waititi Marae in Auckland. This extension has continued into *kura*-secondary colleges and *whare wananga*, or tertiary, institutions.

Although these are very successful education alternatives, not all Maori choose this pathway, and those who are still in the mainstream system suffer from lack of shared values and knowledge, low achievement, and early exit from school. Maori are over represented in statistics of poverty, low educational achievement, suicide, crime, early death, poor health, and mental illness.

Following is the pathway Maori education initiatives have taken thus far. My own pathway was through the mainstream system in a family of a Maori father and *Pakeha* (European) mother. Although my father was a Native speaker, he did not speak Maori at home: even when spoken to he chose to reply in English. It was not until later in his life, as he trained to be a Maori language teacher, that I heard him converse in Maori. The knowledge that he taught other children to speak Maori and not his own, is one of the critical events influencing my education career choices. Other critical events include my masters study at Auckland University in the area of Maori education where critical theory analysis of the current state of Maori educational concerns caused me months of depression. This was only alleviated by the awareness that this depression was a stage in the "emancipation process."

In 1994, I was recruited by Awataha Marae, a *pan-tribal marae* in urban Auckland that delivered education to unemployed youth. These programs are funded by the government on a scholarship basis and offer an opportunity for specialized program development with defined outcomes into employment or further training. My task was to develop the programs for the process and write the document required by the government for Marae to become an accredited education provider. Although the experience of working in a totally Maori system was invigorating and fulfilling, the challenge of mediating between dominant European structures and competing, traditional Maori structures proved very stressful and emotionally painful. This has had enormous impact on my life. I am now teaching part time in a mainstream school and continuing my master's study.

The latest critical event in my life is to unfold here. My vision for an education system that serves indigenous children and youth is best expressed by a poem in a paper written by one of my lecturers, as shown here:

PA HARAKEKE

Tiakina te whanau pa harakeke
(Look after the flax bush whanau)
Tiakina a Rangi raua ko Papa
(Look after Rangi and Papa)
Tiakina to awa
(Look after your river)
Tiakina to maunga
(Look after your mountain)
Tiakina to whanau

(Look after your extended family)
Tiakina to hapu
(Look after your immediate family)
Tiakina to iwi
(Look after your tribe)
Tiakina te rangatahi
(Look after the young ones)
Tiakina nga koroua me nga kuia
(Look after the elderly)
Tiakina te rangimarie me to aroha
(Look after peace and love)
Tiakina te whanau pa harakeke
(Look after the flax bush family)
Kia ora ai te iwi Maori
(So that we, the iwi Maori, may live forever.)

—*Kapua Te Paea Smith*
(age 8, *Te Kaupapa Maori o Maungawhau.*)

Transition II

Path to Native Language and Cultural Revitalization
"Everything you need to know is in the language."

What we learn from Kate, Jeannette, and Linda's models is that Native knowing is very fragile because it exists in indigenous languages and ceremonies that are teetering on the edge of extinction. They argue for Native epistemological significance in which knowledge emerges from the essence of indigenous stories, arts and crafts, songs and chants, and dances. Additionally, this framework is complex and dynamic because it is defined by both traditional and contemporary contexts. We could view the first three models as forwarding an educational framework that is much like nested boxes or nested dolls. Recognizing that knowing is infinitely rich and layered, with each box never empty, and the connection of each box to the other is never linear, but lapping into, through, and out of each other as they move through time and spheres of dynamic relationships.

Yet, we need to be cautious about over-romanticizing a Native educational model. Certainly, there is a great temptation to employ Native values and Native stories as texts for new leadership and organizational models, because it is sexy and it sells. Focusing on the romantic perspective of what appears to an outsider to be Native, dismisses the dismal plight of Native children and youth. It ignores the issue that our Native children and youth must forfeit their cultural heritage, language, ceremonies, and knowledge to participate and to be successful in a contemporary world of hyper reality filled with fast information and rapidly changing technologies.

Jeannette was passionate about what must drive any model of Native learning. In her journal she wrote:

> The thing that each model presented was to give language a priority. To find ways, in whatever way possible, to return the original language to our peoples. Underlining this mission, it seems to me, is a clear statement! That somehow the uniqueness of our tribal identity is contained in our languages. Our language makes clear who we are. Everything you need to know is in the language. This statement holds the power to shape and change the future.
>
> Our Native languages also point to how important, how precious, our diverse Native cultures are. It was apparent that each of our models gained inspiration, information and even guidance from each other. Think of what would happen if we connected and developed a more concrete, collective and comprehensive plan? One of the principles we must embrace is mutual support and we must also understand that at various levels of difference solutions will necessarily be different. Another principle is that we approach learning from within our tribal perspectives and approaches.
>
> We must focus on the students' needs rather than the needs of the society. There seems to be a strong principle around the whole person within the community and its incorporation into the educational values. There is also a strong principle of liberation education and decolonization against competitiveness. Regarding instruction, experiential and discovery processes rather than traditional lecture structured learning is important.

Throughout the gathering, participants discussed the challenges of maintaining culture, language, history, and identity. In addition, the sharing of each model, concrete teaching and learning activities, curriculum, and problem-solving techniques were introduced (please refer to these models for examples, and to the appendix for resources and references). L.A. Napier shared her belief of how Native communities must define their needs:

> Do we know our needs? I think that perhaps we do. The 1970s and 1980s were filled with one study after another; one needs assessment after another. And, in the early 1990s there was a White House Conference on Indian Education and a national report on the status of Indian education, the *Indian Nations at Risk*. I think our true task, and the thrust of our model, is to share knowledge and practices that have been effective and to support one an-

other in our attempts to take action. To take action takes great courage and strength because you take on the risk of being criticized and being wrong. But, I think not to try, not to even attempt is the greater tragedy.

The models presented in this text, and in particular the following four, propose different steps toward culturally responsible pedagogy. For example, the educational leaders suggest that curriculum and instruction emphasize cooperative teaching methods and noncompetitive assessments. Specific examples shared by the Piegan Institute, Oneida Turtle School, and the *kura kaupapa* of Aotearoa suggest interdisciplinary approaches, the use of multicultural and culture-specific literature, and an increased attention on visual and spatial literacy. Through use of the models, the classroom becomes the catalyst for the development of cultural identity and community pride. For Native Hawaiian youth (see Keahi's, chap. 7, & Silva's, chap. 5, models), language preservation has involved them in developing initiatives and academic programs that build cultural pride and self-esteem as well as achieve economic and political self-determination.

Genevieve shared the following from her journal:

> Maenette asked us to write a story of education that embraces all of us. Education was once seen, and for some it still remains, as a punishment. Native children were ripped away from family to be educated. In many public school settings today, Native children do not learn about who they are, so, they believe that who they are does not amount to very much. Native education, however, is filled with symbols, universal truths of spirituality in a place, the role of facilitation in the learning process, and an inclusive vision. I see themes of community, of culture-based learning, and of struggle to define knowledge and universal knowledge that crosses cultures. The Maori's talk of kaupapa as a center. This is a philosophy, an understanding that resonates with many indigenous people. We must take our history, language, and religions to create an energy source. What a beautiful idea that we are all related. We may express ourselves differently, but we can trust our connectedness.

Reprise
by Genevieve Gollnick

I stand on the roof of the lodge
Watching the light on the Western Mountains.
Peace, Tranquillity, Beauty, Life.
In the Western distance, the mountains carry an orange, gold cast.

It is hard to write
Birds wake me
And, I continue seeing them fly.
The sun is about to spark over the eastern crest.
I wait happily with peace.
I heard a cock crow and now
Hens making noisy chatter.
Ready to start the day.
Birds are fortunate to see every morning.

'Elima (Chapter 5)

Advocating for a Stimulating and Language-Based Education: "If you don't learn your language where can you go home to?"

Sarah Keahi
Native Hawaiian Educator

Prologue

The previous three models, presented by Kate, Jeannette, and Linda, articulate the need for a child–youth centered educational vision, grounded on Native principles, language, and culture. In addition, the model calls for the family, the extended family, and the community (both Native and non-Native), to work collaboratively to foster healthy learning environments. Sarah's model supported these ideas and envisions Native children and youth being successful within their own Native language, culture, and diverse academic venues across the global village. To best achieve this, her framework teaches self-sufficiency and cultural esteem that is grounded in Native principles of active family and community participation, Native language, and culture instruction, and learning subject matter that enables youth to both survive and thrive in a modern, dynamic world.

Perhaps the most important lesson that Sarah presents is that an educational leader, in order to actualize any Native educational vision, must first make connections between ideas and groups of people. Throughout her model she links the principles that have guided Native Hawaiian education to the gifts of knowing that other gathering participant's share in their models. Sarah, an active leader in the Native Hawaiian language movement since the 1960s, has experienced the tensions that arise as schools shift from the English language to the Native Hawaiian language, and from Western pedagogies to Native pedagogies. Because these processes have come under close scrutiny by mainstream scholars and the majority culture, Sarah has pressed Native leaders to work together to learn and to share their unique and similar experiences. This dialogue, she believed, can begin to generate Native criteria and strategies that both studies and advances Native pedagogies. Her message clearly reminds leaders that an evaluation of Native learning must be from a Native, not non-Native, paradigm.

My ancestors were grateful, respectful, and appreciative that their island home provided all of the essentials for their existence and survival. They explored their environment and were able to harvest from it the basic necessities for food, shelter, and clothing. They traversed the broad Pacific and brought with them some of these essentials. They were very resourceful and never wasteful. Not only did the *'āina*, the land, and the *kai*, the sea, provide these basic necessities, but they also provided raw materials to embellish their existence as well as provide amusement in the form of music and dance, as well as recreation. For the most part, their society was one built on cooperation rather than competition. Cooperation and interdependence were crucial to survival. They had a thriving culture in these islands since the 1800s. They were totally self-sufficient and independent of the outside world. They relied on their gods and respected the natural elements. Their spiritual world was an integral part of their material world. The two were inseparable. They lived in total harmony with nature and took only what was needed. They were natural conservationists and ecologists. They were well aware of the fact that since the land and the sea provided for their sustenance, to desecrate, contaminate, or pollute them would be their demise. My model illustrates key ideas important to our Native culture that supports the need of Native Hawaiians to utilize our own resources, to help ourselves, to learn our Native Hawaiian language, to become knowledgeable about our ancestors' culture, to become active participants, not merely passive observers, of all things Hawaiian, and to look to ourselves to solve our problems.

Not only must we look inward, but because we now live in a global village, we need to live and learn from each other; we need to be interdependent. Rosalie Medcraft's idea of the global perspective is a significant one because the world is getting smaller and smaller. We, as Native people, need to be able to function in our Native communities and, at the same time, in

Sarah Keahi

Sarah Keahi: Advocation for a language-based education.

the larger mainstream society. Learning to communicate with one another is important. L. A. Napier's model represents to me the ideal situation because communication and articulation are occurring among all the players involved. I have visited schools in the three geographic regions of the Pacific: Micronesia—Nauru, Majuro (Republic of the Marshall Islands); Melanesia—Fiji and the Solomon Islands; and, Polynesia–Tahiti (the Society Islands) and the Cook Islands. I have observed and witnessed active involvement of the community in education. Cooperation and communication are crucial in this model.

In relation to education, one of the key issues facing Native Hawaiians is the issue of self-esteem. The president of Kamehameha Schools (Dr. Michael Chun) articulated this on his arrival at the school. Kamehameha serves Native Hawaiian children. When asked what he felt was a major problem facing Hawaiian youth relative to education, he responded that it was self-esteem. So how do you improve one's self-esteem? The premise is that if you feel good about who you are, you are likely to do well in whatever you undertake. Inherent in feeling good about who you are is the issue of your identity. Many Native Hawaiians of school age and above are not grounded in their Native culture as well as [in] the introduced culture. They are not knowledgeable about their Hawaiian world and they are floundering in the Western world as well. If you can help them become proud of who they are by becoming knowledgeable about their ancestors and their origins, hopefully, they will develop high self-esteem. This will enable them not only to survive, but with a positive attitude to excel. Hopefully, this will transfer to all subjects in school and to other areas of their lives.

I believe that in Hawai'i, the Hawaiian language immersion program has increased Native Hawaiian children's self-esteem. Immersion is not without its problems, but one only has to observe a class in action or an activity in progress to come to that realization—that it is working. The faces of the children reveal the success of the program and national standardized test scores have verified this. The immersion program is Native Hawaiian and is language-based. As indigenous educators, we know that a culture and its language are inseparable for the language is the vehicle by which the culture is transmitted.

Language is a priority. Darrell Kipp's model was similar to mine because of the priority given to the language. In language, we find our identity and the very essence of our existence. When I first looked at his model, I wondered about the dollar signs on the yellow blocks. After he explained I thought, "That's interesting, all we need is money to build our buildings and provide furnishings and we can do the rest!" In Hawai'i, we have made use of existing buildings such as church halls and schools.

In 1896, the Hawaiian language was outlawed as a language of instruction. It was in 1996 that our organization, the 'Ahahui 'Ōlelo Hawai'i, spoke with Hawai'i's governor about declaring 1996 the Year of Hawaiian Language. I encourage my students to learn other languages, but I teach them that Hawaiian is the language of their home. They can go anywhere to study foreign languages. Go to Japan and learn Japanese, learn Spanish or French, but if you don't learn your mother language here, there is no where you can go to learn it! So, we Hawaiians and teachers of Hawaiian language have an obligation to our people, our culture, and our homeland to perpetuate our language. This sense of urgency is real to us as we witness, daily, the passing away of our Native speakers many of which include our great grandparents, grandparents, and others. There are fewer and fewer every year.

Our *kūpuna* (elders) are very important to us. Sam Suina's model was clear and profound. The attention to the ancestors and the natural elements are so central to his people. This is like my people. Our kūpuna are held in high regard for they are the source and they are our teachers. They are the keepers of our traditions. They have the wisdom and we are the beneficiaries of their legacy. And, it is our responsibility to pass this legacy on to our children and grandchildren.

Along with my model, I added a few newspaper articles from our local newspapers that I thought would provide evidence to support my model. The articles include: "Hawaiian Studies Needed" "Laws Protect Language Rights," and "Ānuenue Immersed in Hawaiian." Ānuenue is O'ahu's first Hawaiian immersion school for Grades K–12. It has a sister school on the Big Island called Nāwahīokalaniopu'u. The fourth article is entitled "Hawaiian Language College-born." The University of Hawai'i at Hilo will house the first Hawaiian Language College. It will be the third school at the university, in addition to arts and sciences, and agriculture. The college will offer several degree programs in Hawaiian-related fields including the first graduate degree for an indigenous language offered anywhere in the nation. We are proud and excited about it.

We need to develop more teaching tools and materials. Teachers across the state continually work on this. Some of my friends and colleagues have been working on textbooks, posters, audiotapes, videotapes and other curriculum needs. We have few resources, and have to produce our own materials. Hawaiian language proponents and teachers have been doing this work. We are also working on curriculum development at Kamehameha.

We currently have a required Hawaiian history and Hawaiian culture course for graduation and a 5-year Hawaiian-language offering. We offer courses in Hawaiian chant, dance, and arts and crafts. We also need to think about how to incorporate practical skills into our teaching. Jeannette Armstrong's model was very complex. She related that one of the key issues in her community is providing practical skills for some of their at-risk students.

As an educational leader I feel rewarded, frustrated and challenged, but what I have learned to do is to observe the Ahs! and the Ahahs! We look for them in young people and within ourselves. I experienced Ahs! and Ahahs! after hearing each participant's model presentation. Some key elements that stand out in my mind about Native education are that it needs to be holistic, embracing the mind, body and spirit. Additionally, the experience must be positive and language-based. We need to know that we can do it ourselves. That is, we need to draw on the resources and expertise in our Native communities, and especially, from our elders. Finally, all work must be passionate and dynamic. Whatever we do we must move forward collectively and do what is honorable to our elders and ancestors. In closing, there are two Hawaiian 'ōlelo no'eau or wise sayings that come to mind. I share them with you as follows:

"Ehele wāwae kākou, e like me ko kākou kūpuna me ke kapukapu a me ka ha'aheo"
(Let us walk like our ancestors with dignity and pride)
"Emālama 'ia nā pono o ka 'āina e nā 'ōpio"
(The traditions of the land are perpetuated by its youth).

'Eono (Chapter 6)

A Commitment to Language-Based Education: *"Among the gifts we can give our children is our cultural traditions."*

Darrell Kipp
The Piegan Institute

Prologue

There is a sense of urgency in the tenor of the participants' voices as they share their individual models. Darrell captures this emotion eloquently. He argued, in lucid language, that the intrusion of Western ways of knowing has led Native populations to develop an unreasonable dependency on colonial structures and institutions. Over time, this has resulted in the casting away of Native traditions and the loss of language, culture, and respect for Native knowledge. Darrell pointed to the experience of the Pikuni (Piegan) tribe of the Blackfoot Confederacy (consisting of Kainah, Pikuni, and Siksika). The reality of losing their Native language and cultural identity became clear as the number of Native-speaking elders began to dwindle. Would the Pikuni become the next indigenous culture to lose their connection to their ancestors?

This question, Darrell explained, required an indigenous educational model to establish a covenant between the school and the community to promote Native language, culture, and tribal protocol instruction. Most importantly, Darrell insisted, to sustain Native language-based education Native and non-Native institutions must recognize tribal sovereignty and genuine power of Native members of the community to make educational decisions. The sustainability of the model, he argued, is further enhanced by the substance of the learning experiences. He called for crafting a critical, unique, language-based curriculum that is taught by Native teachers in a supportive, nurturing educational environment. Although Darrell acknowledged that tribes will approach education in different ways, he argued that all learning and teaching must be both "a mirror to the past and a torch to the future."

Darrell Kipp

BACKGROUND

I started teaching many years ago; first as an English professor and teacher in my own community and in many Indian communities. I taught what would be considered English 101: GED. I have also had the privilege of teaching graduate-level courses in English. I never thought I would be able to do that when I first started because when I first went to college I could not pass the basic English entrance exam.

Visiting my home on the Blackfoot Indian Reservation in 1978, I was asked to teach a class in an extension program. The class was Psychology

101. Teaching the class, it became clear that the students were not able to read or write on an acceptable level. I studied the members of the class, and although I had been away from home for quite awhile, it seemed to me they represented the college strata of the community. Most were not suffering any serious hardships and most had graduated from high school with a diploma, but it was clear they could barely read and write on even an eighth grade level. From that time on, I was aware of the "fallacy" of education.

In 1982, having worked most of my life as a technical writer and teaching part time, I took a degree, a master's in fine arts in poetry. At that time, I thought it would enhance my ability to teach primarily Native children the ability to communicate. In subsequent years, I was always astounded by the incongruity, the contradiction, the dichotomy of having roomfuls of good looking, intelligent people in front of me with a total lack of ability, of skill, or of training to write even the simplest paragraph. I have always thought, and still do, that Native American education suffers an enormous amount because the majority of the students lack the ability to read and write at acceptable levels.

In 1986, teaching again at a college, a colleague and I experimented off the cuff. We offered a course in Blackfoot Language 101. One group took both Blackfoot and English 101. They did better than other groups. Since that time, it's been a long involved journey toward trying to find the optimal way to teach in our own language. I'm not a linguist, I'm not an anthropologist, and I'm not a militant. I'm none of these things. I'm an educator. If educators do not constantly seek to define and fine tune their teaching abilities so they teach at their optimal level, they are a disgrace to their profession. We (at the Piegan Institute) actually work best with teachers that do not have teaching degrees. This allows us to teach them. Teachers with degrees want to line up the desks in rows.

MY MODEL FOR EDUCATION

This model is a localized one, and is very close to me. In my work I've found that I'm barely able to speak for myself and barely able to validate for my family. I have to really struggle to validate (small laugh) for my own tribe, and certainly would never be so presumptuous as to speak for all Native peoples. But when we were sitting here (during the interview), I heard the bell ring, and I recalled the familiar phrase, "No man is an island, every man is a piece of the continent, part of the main land, and any man's death diminishes me because I am involved in all mankind. Never presume to know,

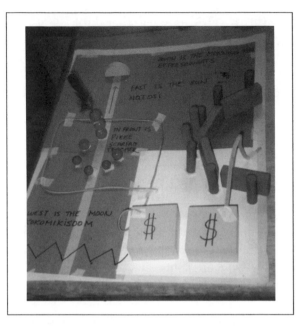

Darrell Kipp's *A Commitment to Language-Based Education*.

therefore, for whom the bell tolls. It tolls for thee." I believe that in this day and age, when we talk about the death of Native languages, we're talking about diminishing the world. Any time a language disappears, or ceases to exist, it diminishes me as a person. When we lose things like that I think it diminishes all of us. So, one of the things I did in my brief model was to stress harmony and cooperation.

Our own model is a cooperative one. One of the most destructive elements you can have in a school is competitiveness. Competitiveness really destroys our sense of community. It destroys a family and it destroys cohesion. One of the things that Indian people, and particularly my tribe, suffer from is a great deal of *fragmentation*. A lot of people and a lot of things create that fragmentation today. In my model, I wanted to first build a very powerful fence. It puts up an obstacle. I consider my tribe, and I think of other tribes, I consider ours under siege. Not a moment passes when Native people are not besieged by some group or someone. Someone is going to do something to us, do something good for us. You think of the phrase, "this will be good for you." I remember my mother, who was not a violent woman, would occasionally, when I was misbehaving, take a pancake turner out of the drawer and wave it at me like she was going to strike me and say, "This will be good for you."

Many things that were brought to Indian people were not brought to destroy them. They were brought in the name of love. What people thought their love would do for us, in fact, killed us. So, I would say that one of the things in my model is we build strong walls and we try to keep certain things out. We're desperate to keep certain influences away from us. We ask, "Could you leave us alone for just a little while? Just give us a break. Just back off and leave us alone until we can get our health back, until we can get our strength back, until we can get our own vision back." There are times when the strongest language is silence.

I believe one of the things that we desperately need to build into our model is very strong walls. For example, in our immersion schools, we have a "no-visitor" policy, although this runs counter to Indian people and hospitality. The trouble was that we allowed people to come in and they would not adhere to our rule of no English spoken in the building. They would come in and say, "Oh, what nice little children. Oh, come over here." We'd say, "Please, please, no English." And they wouldn't do it. So we locked the doors, and said, "That's it. I'm sorry. You can't come in here anymore." Indian people are so accommodating that we hurt ourselves with our own accommodation. Now, if you allow accommodation in an immersion school, you'll ruin the immersion school. You'll never get anywhere. So, you can't have it happen, so you build a wall. No one come inside this building unless they speak the language, and if they refuse, they can't come in.

We've had some very touch-and-go situations over this rule. A very influential woman from our community, a member of our tribe, came to visit the school. She is a fluent speaker and one of the big skeptics. We have a rule, we say, "Make a friend out of a skeptic. Make a friend out of a critic." And we work very hard at that. We invited her to our school to have lunch with us. We admonished her, "Please, don't use English because it just doesn't work." However, during lunch, for whatever her reasons, she chose not to use our tribal language. She chose to speak in English with the children much to our dismay. At the end of the meal, one of the little boys told her, "You're not an Indian, are you?" She said, "What! Of course I am." The boy again said, "You're not an Indian." "What makes you think that?" "You never spoke any Indian since you came." That confirmed for me, in many ways, that language is so powerful a part of identity.

Because the sun rises in the east, our schools are built so that every morning, as we open the doors to our schools, the first entity, the first sacred person we meet, is our father the sun. The four entities we are particularly concerned with in education are the sun, and our mother, the moon. The sun and moon's son, who rises with his father, is the morning star, and the one who intervened, and worked to bring the gifts we have today, is darkness. Scarface, the first teacher, is still with us. We do not buy the theory that Indian people came over the Bering Strait. We know from stories of our origin that we were *put* here. Archeological fact proves that we've been here for 9,000 years. Long ago, we were in a very cold world, and Scarface went to live with the sun. When he went to the sun, the sun taught him to build four sweat lodges. When he was doing it, a star would come out, then disappear. After he built the fourth sweat lodge, and the star was gone, the sun told Scarface to return to the earth via the Wolf's tail, the Milky Way. Scarface returned, and shared all he had learned with the people. This belief gives us our power and our religion. We strongly base our schools and our thinking on the teachings of Scarface.

We also use sign language a lot in our schools; we also use a technique called *brain stitching*, that has a lot to do with self-esteem. We did a lot of research on body language. We went into the public schools to work with the Native children. We wanted to determine the factors for their inability to go to school. We would begin by asking them if they would answer our questions and most said, "Yeah." Before we started, we said, "Oh, by the way, are you an Indian?" They showed a body action, a negative response to being Indian). We called this action the "plug your nose and cover your fly" response. This response developed into the brain stitching technique, that incorporated sign language. We made our hands into a fist and we did not allow pointing (that signals the self), then, toward another person in the group, and then wave the hand in a circle). We were saying, "Me, you, all of us. We're spotted wolves. We're *Pikuni.*" This is our name. We're not Blackfeet. Blackfeet is a name that was given to us by a Board of Indian Affairs (BIA) clerk in 1936. Then we would ask the child, "Now, who are you? What are you?" And the child would say, "I am Pikuni." Very good, very good.

We wanted our schools to be high quality buildings, and they are. They are extremely beautiful buildings and they are not inexpensive. The schools have open spaces because we want the kids to be able to move around. We tell them, "Stand up, walk, turn around, jump. Put your hands on your head." They often get up and dance by themselves. We have three large tables in the room. These three tables are the only furniture we have in the schools. People come to our school, and they say, "Oh, you poor things. You only have three tables." Well, we believe that it's better to have these children move around. The nemesis of learning is to have a child sit still and not move. We allow children to move about, to run.

I want to share that the notion about money management is quite true. We at the Piegan Institute have a financial situation where we do not take money from the government. This means we don't have to ask permission and we don't have to jump through hoops. We don't have to do anything. We can do as we wish. We rely heavily on friendships and generosity. We believe language is powerful. We believe that our language is alive and will take care of us if we continue to be friends with those that go along with our beliefs. We use the analogy that our language is our grandparents, and we tell others, "If you were walking down the road, and your grandparents were sitting alongside the road, would you walk past them? And, if you do walk past them, then you are truly a brutal person, brutal as the rest of the world." We don't want to be like that. We want to remain the ones that stop and care for the grandparent. We then say, "Because we talk of self-sufficiency, of our energies and own abilities, we will never be able to prove those abilities if we allow someone else to dictate to us how to behave. The only thing we can ever ask from the outside is money." Pure and simple, money. We don't need anything else. We don't need computers. We don't need technologies. We don't need other's paradigms. We don't need any of that stuff because what it brings is a whole series of "permission slips" you must sign. If someone truly wants to assist they will give money with no strings attached. If they want strings attached, we do not take it.

One thing I may have indicated is the poverty that I see around us, financial poverty. If you look at statistics (as we are all so familiar with doing) Native Americans are often listed with horrific statistics in the U.S. What if you are the worst off of that group? We have to remind ourselves that there are categories of Native American communities, with some people a little more stable than others, and some literally on the brink of destruction. I worry that the elements of destruction are so powerful we may be in the process of self-annihilation.

I think, however, that when you have so little money that when you do get it, you are so appreciative of every penny that you utilize it for maximum benefit. In our schools, when the first money comes to us, we do not spend it. We put it in an account. Later, we transfer the money in a fellowship account for poor children. We charge tuition to come to our school. Some people think this is outrageous because we are one of the poorest communities in the world. Nevertheless, we charge tuition. We do it because we want the children's parents to have a strong sense of loyalty to the school. If they can only pay $5, that's fine, but they have to realize that they do have to pay. It must be an obligation to fulfill on their part.

I think the most crucial thing for a Native American child, any child, but especially the Native child, is that they have high language acquisition skills. At a very early age, they must be given neurological incentive and training and physiological development. I'm talking strictly about brain, neurological, and physiological development that can be achieved through exposure to multiple language formats. This must be done at an early age. Young children must be introduced to language, sounds of language, and multiple languages. We have to overlook society's rule to only speak one language. Young children that learn in immersion schools without the presence of English have enormously high language acquisition skills. If we can introduce language to children at a profound and intense level, particularly when the child is between the ages of three through six, we can get these children to the point where the acquisition of English, or any language, is simple to them. If we don't do this, I don't think we'll ever change anything.

At one time, there was no one in our community under age 60 that could speak our language. Our language was just about gone. Our tribe in Canada still has 20-year-olds who can speak their language fluently. They are in a much different position than we are because of the U.S.–Canadian border. There is northern Pikuni and southern Pikuni; the separation is due to the border drawn between us. We're all the same people. Our brothers and sisters backed up their horses and stayed in Canada, whereas we stayed in the south. The northern group are in different circumstances because of the way both countries have dealt with their different tribes. There is a very powerful drive in the U.S. to assimilate tribes, and perhaps this was done to a lesser degree in Canada, or they didn't attack the languages as hard as they did in the U.S. When we started the Institute, there was no one around that could speak the language. Those from Canada, because we are relatives and friends, left their homes and families and moved in with us, to teach us. They got our schools started, and we picked up the lessons as fast as we could. Teachers like myself and colleagues had to relearn the language as quickly as we could. We brought older people into the schools. Because teachers with degrees, although they spoke the language, were so indoctrinated in the western model, we had to ask them to leave. They were destroying our culture. We say, "Why is it that our parents didn't speak the language and didn't teach the language to us?" Our parents said they did not teach us the language because they loved us and didn't want us to be harassed, like they had been. If we truly love our parents, and if we truly love our people, we can reconcile that. We can reconcile it, and we can now begin to make up for it.

'Ehiku (Chapter 7)

Revitalizing Culture and Language: "Returning to the 'Āina (land)."

Kalena Silva
University of Hawai'i at Hilo

Prologue

A prevalent theme across each of the models if presented in this volume is the importance of land; a place where Native communities can practice their cultural traditions, raise their children and youth to cherish a rich heritage, and realize a culturally appropriate future. In this chapter, Kalena adds his voice to this message. His model reminds both Native leaders and community members that only through strong community advocacy can social injustices be addressed. He writes that the individual must first embrace the Hawaiian language and culture. When a like-minded group of knowledgeable individuals are drawn together, that group forms a bond born out of respect for their land, lineage, language, and culture. It is this bond that links them to their ancestors as well as to future generations.

The power of the collective wisdom of this group, extended by a knowledge of Hawaiian history, can move communities to effectively address unjust situations and toward renewed action to revitalize Hawaiian ways of knowing and language. Kalena reminds us, once again, that this work can only be done if there is a place, 'āina (land), to do it. In many ways, Kalena echoes the themes presented by Jeannette Armstrong, that the land is connected to community building, Native language preservation, and cultural revitalization.

Kalena writes passionately about the need to teach the Hawaiian language. In this chapter, he traces the near-death of the Hawaiian language in the mid-1980s, to its increasing vitality today. By situating the Hawaiian language movement in an historical context, one is confronted with the themes of assimilation policies, damaging historical stereotypes, and the dilemma of non-Native teachers teaching Native children. This description of colonialism is similar to those told by other Native leaders in this book. The importance of Kalena's story, for educators and policy makers, is how he describes Hawai'i's current effort to re-establish the Native Hawaiian language in K–16+ institutions.

The gift of Kalena's message is the strength of his cultural understanding, eloquence, and clarity of expression. Similar to the ideas shared by Armstrong, Kalena provides the reader with an epistemological taxonomy that is clearly embedded in Native Hawaiian knowing. His use of metaphor supports the holistic nature of learning that links the spirit, mind, and body. His story is a valuable lesson to scholars and practitioners involved in K–12 and in higher education, to policymakers, and all those committed to the revitalization of Native language and culture.

Kalena Silva

THE *NIU* AS METAPHOR FOR THE REVITALIZA-TION OF HAWAIIAN LANGUAGE AND CULTURE

In Hawai'i, the ubiquitous *niu*, the coconut tree, can be used in a great variety of useful ways—for shelter, food, musical instruments, even children's toys. The *niu* is also the physical embodiment of Kū, one of four major Hawaiian deities. The *nui* grows well in our fertile island soil, sending up a trunk topped by spreading leaves, that cradle clusters of the tree's fruit. Although it grows upright, the long, slender trunk of the *niu* bends and sways resiliently in the wind, often surviving major hurricanes even when other trees cannot.

Like the *niu*, our language and culture provide physical, spiritual, and emotional sustenance the strength of which depends on the richness of the soil where it grows. The linguistic and cultural soil in Hawai'i today is becoming increasingly rich as more people recognize the value of the efforts directed toward Hawaiian language and culture revitalization. The increasingly rich soil promotes better fruit, as reflected in the growing strength of Hawaiian language and culture. We have learned not to just survive but to flourish we, like the *niu*, must be resilient, bending and swaying, yet remain ever upright.

Kalena Silva's *Revitalizing Culture and Language.*

HAWAIIAN IMMERSION EDUCATION
AT THE UNIVERSITY OF HAWAI'I AT HILO

One of the guiding principles of Hawaiian language education at the University of Hawai'i at Hilo (UHH) is found in the words, *'O ka 'ōlelo ke kā'a."* Literally, *Language binds like ornamental cordage.* Traditionally, this cordage, *ke ka'ā,* is painstakingly lashed in intricate patterns to bind the lures of certain types of fishing lines. Simultaneously, as *ke ka'ā* serves the utilitarian function of holding together a survival tool, it also serves an aesthetic function in the intricacy and beauty of its execution. Similarly, a language binds its speakers together in ways that are both prosaic and poetic, commonplace and aesthetically appealing. Hawaiian language education at UHH has sought, since its inception in the late 1970s, to strengthen these levels of Hawaiian language use in communities statewide.

In the following remarks, I present a brief historical context that includes several major events that led to the decline of the Hawaiian language. I comment on the increasing vitality of Hawaiian in communities statewide since the early 1980s and on the role of UHH's Hawaiian Studies program in this increasing vitality. I will also describe recent state legislative actions mandating organizational change at UHH to provide support for the growth of Hawaiian language education, and present a summary of the philosophical statement recently developed by a group of Hawaiian language educators regarding issues of education and identity.

Although changes due to foreign influences began with the arrival of the first foreigners in 1778, Hawaiian language and culture have suffered a great and continuous decline since 1820, when New England Calvinist missionaries began actively converting Hawaiians to Christianity. The Hawaiian language continued to be spoken by most Hawai'i residents—Hawaiian and non-Hawaiian alike—until the end of the 19th century, when political developments led to the overthrow of the Hawaiian monarchy in 1893. Three years later, a law was passed by the Republic of Hawai'i that made illegal the use of Hawaiian as a language of instruction in the schools. As English then became the sole legal language of instruction and the only language permitted spoken on school grounds, students on all the islands, with the exception of Ni'ihau, were forced to abandon the Hawaiian language. In 1898, the annexation of Hawai'i by the United States effectively took away all opportunities for Hawaiian political self-determination and reaffirmed the prevailing legal status of English. In 1900, Hawai'i became a U.S. territory, and in 1959, the 50th state in the union. These dramatic political, social, and linguistic changes, combined with the influence of immigrant sugar and pineapple plantation laborers from foreign countries (e.g., China, Japan, the Philippines), resulted in the decline of Hawaiian language use and gave rise to Hawai'i Creole English, commonly called "pidgin English" in Hawai'i today.

After the turn of the century, the decline in the number of Hawaiians who were knowledgeable in traditional language and culture was matched by a concomitant rise of those who embraced the English language and the Euro-American culture. Although all of the estimated 40,000 Hawaiians at the turn of the century spoke Hawaiian, by the late 1970s, only some 2,000 Native speakers remained.

Fortunately, in the mid-1960s, a widespread renewed interest in Hawaiian language and culture had emerged and was reflected in growing student enrollments and in the increasing rigor applied to Hawaiian language study at the University of Hawai'i at Mānoa. Bachelor of arts degrees in Hawaiian language and Hawaiian studies were established at the Mānoa campus in 1978. None of UHH's present Hawaiian studies faculty pursued a bachelor' degree in Hawaiian language, instead earning degrees in other fields. However, all faculty completed Mānoa's Hawaiian language program, which included 4 years of Hawaiian as a second language. Immersion education glimmered faintly on the horizon, especially at the junior and senior levels of language study, but had not yet been fully implemented.

In 1978, Edith Kanaka'ole, who had been offering Hawaiian language and culture courses at UHH for several years, sought the help of William H. "Pila" Wilson to develop a course of study that led to the BA in Hawaiian studies at the Hilo campus. Pila had completed the 4-year Hawaiian language study at Mānoa and was completing the PhD in linguistics there. The two-track BA program Pila developed with Mrs. Kanaka'ole and her daughter, Pua Kanahele, also a teacher at UHH, focused specifically on Hawaiian music, dance, literature, linguistics, and traditional culture. The program is taught solely through the medium of Hawaiian at the junior and senior levels and in selected courses at the freshman and sophomore levels. UHH's BA in Hawaiian studies was first awarded to graduates in 1982. The program has experienced extraordinary growth in the past 15 years, from some 10 student majors in 1982 to over 100 in 1998.

This unprecedented growth is due in large part to a mounting interest among students, generated by the increasingly high public profile of Hawaiian immersion education. Outside the university setting, such education is now being offered principally at the nonprofit Pūnana Leo preschools, established in 1983, and at the Hawai'i state department of education's Hawaiian Immersion program for elementary and secondary public school students, Ka Papahana Kaiapuni Hawai'i. The Ka Papahana Kaiapuni Hawai'i program was established in 1987 after a prohibiting Hawaiian language instruction in public schools was finally rescinded, and in response to Pūnana Leo families who made strong, incessant appeals to legislators and educators for the continuation of their children's Hawaiian immersion education into the elementary and secondary levels.

Initially, state agencies gave little moral and no financial support for Hawaiian immersion education, expressing unsubstantiated fears that students' ability to master English would be impaired. Additionally, the agencies severely underestimated the quality of education that could be provided. Over the years, the unwavering commitment and dogged tenacity of the families of immersion school students has won increasing support among legislators and educators, many of whom have come to realize that there is a moral obligation to perpetuate a language in its homeland. As a result, some state financial support has been provided for Ka Papahana Kaiapuni Hawai'i, although the support is far from adequate. The Pūnana Leo continues to receive no state government financial support and relies solely on federal government grants and donations from private entities.

Despite the obstacles, the number of Kula Kaiapuni students continues to grow. In the fall of 1998, some 1,500 students, from kindergarten through Grade 12, were enrolled in Kula Kaiapuni classes, thereby requiring an increase in the pool of trained teachers and the expansion of curriculum development. UHH's Hawaiian language faculty have sought to address these critical shortages and other separate, yet related, issues of Hawaiian education at the University level in several ways. I outline next some of the major developments.

In July 1997, Governor Benjamin Cayetano signed into law the establishment of a Hawaiian language college at UHH. The University's board of regents approved renaming the college, Ka Haka 'Ula O Ke'elikōlani (The venerable standard of Ke'elikōlani) after the 19th century Hawaiian Princess Ke'elikōlani, a steadfast supporter of Hawaiian language and culture who demanded, sources reveal, that only Hawaiian be spoken in her presence. Ka Haka 'Ula O Ke'elikōlani provides the larger organizational structure that our programs, most of which have been in place for some years now, can find a single home.

One such program is the Hale Kuamo'o Hawaiian Language Center, established by the Hawai'i state legislature in 1989. The center supports and encourages the expansion of the Hawaiian language as a medium of communication in education, business, government and other contexts of social life in the public and private sectors of Hawai'i and beyond. The Hale Kuamo'o serves as the center for the development of instructional materials for Kula Kaiapuni students statewide. It is also responsible for reaching out to involve indigenous language scholars, maintaining the college's Polynesian language database, maintaining the permanent secretariat of the Polynesian languages forum, and performing outreach work in communities in and outside Hawai'i, among other responsibilities.

Until recently, Hale Kuamo'o also provided Kula Kaiapuni inservice teacher training. Such training is now provided by a program housed in the Hawaiian Language College: A Hawaiian medium teacher education program, that addresses the specific and unique language and cultural requirements of a Kula Kaiapuni classroom. This experimental program is now completing a self-study for submission to, and approval by, the department of education. Once approved, it will exist apart from, but in communication with, the existing English medium education program at UHH.

Students in the Hawaiian medium teacher education program gain practical teaching and curriculum development experience at the college's laboratory school, Nāwahīokalani'ōpu'u, with students in Grades 7 through 12. Most of the nearly 80 students at Nāwahīokalani'ōpu'u are graduates of the Pūnana Leo preschool. One of only two Hawai'i public schools where all classes are taught through the medium of Hawaiian, Nāwahīokalani'ōpu'u school will graduate its first class in 1999. Together with the state department of education and private schools, Nāwahīokalani'ōpu'u school works closely with the Office of Hawaiian Affairs, the 'Aha Pūnana Leo and the federal government.

Another Hawaiian Language College program, Hawaiian studies, delivers a BA in Hawaiian Studies, an MA in Hawaiian Language and Literature, a minor and certificate in Hawaiian Studies, and a certificate in Hawaiian Language. The MA, that began with nine students in the fall of 1998, is the first, and at present, the only, Hawaiian language graduate program in existence. A future program associated with Hawaiian studies is liberal education, to provide a broad-based program for students who enter UHH from Hawaiian medium schools or who have particularly strong Hawaiian cultural backgrounds.

As one would correctly assume, several of the college's programs have taken years to be approved. The MA in Hawaiian language and literature—a case in point—took 5 years to be approved, and even after approval, was postponed for 1 year due to the external accreditation review process. Progress toward administrative approval of programs often occurs very slowly or in spurts. Of course, even after approval is finally received, the programs only provide the organizational framework for the real work of actual implementation.

The programs of UHH's Hawaiian Language College have enjoyed some success in immersion education. Our programs have been described as the most innovative, and as the only ones developed in Native American language to be found anywhere in the United States. The frequent visits of those interested in language revitalization from around the world are a reflection of our success.

Yet, it is clear that we have a very long way to go. We are not there yet. The question of where "there" is, that is, what we'd like to see Hawaiian immersion programs at all levels ultimately accomplish over the long-term, was grappled with early in 1998 by a group of Hawaiian language educators. To ensure a wide representation of ideas, the group was comprised of both Native and non-Native speakers of Hawaiian, and spanned three generations who came from all levels of Hawaiian immersion education, from preschool to university levels.

Early in our group retreats, held over a period of several weekends, we agreed that although language revitalization is essential, it is but one of several major, interrelated elements. By March 1998, our group developed the first draft, in Hawaiian, of its philosophical statement, *Ke Kumu Honua Mauli ola*, which I translate very tentatively as the Foundation of Contexts Conducive to the Expression of Identity. The statement abounds with language and terms rich in Hawaiian cultural meaning and nuances, not easily explained in English, and beyond the scope of this chapter. Without question, a full understanding of the statement can only be obtained from the original Hawaiian. Nonetheless, because I believe that it provides a philosophical template for the future direction of Hawaiian immersion education, and contains universal elements that may be useful in other cultural contexts, I present a summary.

At the core of the philosophy's foundation lies the *mauli Hawai'i*, the unique life force which is cultivated by, emanates from, and distinguishes a person who identifies themself as a Hawaiian. If tended properly, this *mauli*, like a well-tended fire, can burn brightly. If not, like a neglected fire, it can die out. Four major elements of an individual's life-giving *mauli* are identified in relationship to the parts of the body where they are tended:

1. *Ka 'Ao'ao Pili 'Uhane*—the spiritual element, that is, the spirit with which we are all born; and which is seated in the head, the most sacred part of the body, that recognizes right from wrong, good from bad, and that creates a relationship with everything in the universe, both seen and unseen.

2. *Ka 'Ao'ao 'Ōlelo*—the language element found in the ears, the mouth, and the tongue. Language can be used in many different ways, and may be soft, rough, gentle, harsh, forthright, or secretive, but perhaps its greatest strength lies in its ability to transmit mauli to future generations.

3. *Ka 'Ao'ao 'Ike Ku'una*—the traditional knowledge element seated in the intestines, where knowledge and emotions lie, and that is expressed in traditional values and practices, like the hula, poetry, and prayer. Such practices have creative aspects, and, like language, can reflect misrepresentations. Thus, the true power in traditional knowledge lies in authentic practices carried out by mature people who recognize their cultural responsibility to others who share their *mauli*.

4. *Ka 'Ao'ao Lawena*—the physical behavior element found in the limbs of the body, in gestures, in the way one stands, in the way one moves the feet when walking, in a facial expression, in a smile. This element of one's *mauli* is usually learned through unconscious imitation at a young age, and thus, is easily recognized and appreciated by those who share the same *mauli*.

In addition to the four elements of *mauli*, which are tended within an individual's body, there are three elements of *mauli* shared by a group of people that connect them to the divine, to preceding generations, and to generations to come. Found in three centers of the body, they are the:

1. Piko 'Ī—the fontanel at the top of our heads when we are babies and through which we became physically connected to the spiritual beliefs of our people.
2. Piko 'Ō—the navel, attached to the umbilical cord and placenta, that connects us to our ancestors, and is closest to the *na'au*, the seat of our knowledge and emotions.
3. *Piko 'Ā*—the reproductive organs which create future generations, and by extension, all we create and establish.

Through these three centers, we exist in relation to one another as members of a group of people among whom are shared the elements of spirit, language, traditional knowledge, and physical behavior. Lastly, *mauli* cannot survive if there are not also *honua*, places where we may freely express our *mauli*. Even as the *mauli Hawai'i* has been weakened greatly over the years, we can seek to create *honua* within our families, among friends, at school, at work, and in other places where the fires of our *mauli* may be rekindled and once again burn brightly.

In summary, despite major events in Hawaiian history that have caused a great decline in Hawaiian language and culture, the emergence in the 1970s of a renewed interest in things Hawaiian led, in the 1980s, to the establishment of Hawaiian language immersion education at the preschool, elementary, secondary, and tertiary levels. The several programs of UHH's newly established Hawaiian Language College play a leading, statewide role in language revitalization efforts. A philosophical statement developed recently by Hawaiian language educators affirms the importance of *mauli*, the combination of interrelated elements that are the source of one's identity and worldview.

You may recall that at the beginning of this chapter, I quoted the words which have served as a major guiding principle for Hawaiian language education at UHH, *'O ka 'ōlelo ke ka'ā*. Remembering the value of those words, we would be wise now to consider the full implications of the words, *'O ka mauli ke ka'ā*.

'Ewalu (Chapter 8)

Building an Indigenous Language Center:
"The children have the right to learn their language."

Gail Kiernan
Ministry of Justice, Perth, Australia

Prologue

What becomes clear in Gail Kiernan's contribution to our learning is the actual and painful effect of racism directed toward indigenous people. Although Gail's dream for a place where both Aboriginal and non-Aboriginal people can meet, share stories, and learn Aboriginal languages and cultures is rich with hope and passion, she described her dream with a guarded optimism. Like Darrell Kipp, Gail is also enraged by the effects of colonialism and racial division on generations of Native people. She acknowledges that in Australia, current governing attitudes are still oppressive toward Aborigines, and that this attitude builds political barriers that make work toward social justice difficult. The long-lasting effect of this oppression has enforced the colonial mindset of disempowerment and hopelessness. Many elders, Gail observes, evidence this in their negative reactions to their political activism by Aboriginal individuals and groups. It is because of the long-term effects of the colonial mindset, Gail asserts, that Native leaders must work diligently to create more just social climates and to move Aboriginal people toward sovereign action.

What is also compelling about Gail's work is her current efforts to teach the Aboriginal language and culture to the most disenfranchised—women in the prison system. Although her work in this area to build community and to empower women is certainly at the cutting edge, Gail understands that it also challenges institutional power structures. Creating long-lasting attitudinal and institutional change within Native communities and between Native and non-Native borders is hard work. For those who undertake such a labor, it is a lifelong battle. What is remarkable is that every educational leader involved in In Our Mother's Voice is also an institutional change agent. Leadership, as illuminated in Gail's dream, is a process that directs and motivates purposeful action toward social justice, equity, and change.

I believe I am a most fortunate woman at this time in my life. I am committed to maintaining and renewing my people's language and culture for future generations. The joys of being able to help Aboriginal children to be able to learn (building trust, acceptance, and understanding between teacher and student) have been great. I am grateful to be able to help my people in any way I am able. The challenges in my life have been contributing factors that have led me along the path to where I am today. A challenge in my life was returning to school at age 33 to gain the high school education I never received as a child. I found the courage and confidence to complete my teaching certificate in secondary education. After receiving a position in a primary school, I remember wondering if I had the strength and confidence to work in an educational institution, as I had very negative feelings from the past regarding education. I taught there for 5 years. At that time, I became aware of the need for language and culture teachings. More recently, I have moved into the unknown, the justice system, where I am today.

THE DREAM

In Western Australia, we desperately need to have something to revive the language and culture, to maintain it and bring it back again because we have lost so much. It's my dream to have a huge, global building that people can feel good about coming to. Young people could learn about the past from the old, who could work there as well. They could study for the future and eventually connect to an indigenous language center in Australia itself.

I used silver on the top of my model because in a lot of our traditional paintings and body painting, in the past as well as now, white, light, or silver represents a sacred or spiritual thing. I imagine that the top place would

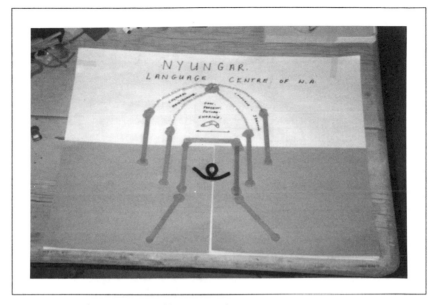

Gail Kieran's *Building an Indigenous Language Center.*

have that feeling. The boomerang and the spear are a part of the top because they are also ceremonial objects that we still treasure today. We have ceremonies where we bury them, in cities or near rivers, and we don't put a mark there because we don't want people to come along and take it. We don't want it to be a tourist sort of event. I'm learning because I'm with the older people now. They're starting to share their stories with me. I used orange in the model because it is my favorite color, a happy, positive color. And, I used green because most people identify southwestern Australia as very green. It's mostly rainforest and has some of the oldest trees in the world. It's where I come from.

The part in the middle of the model represents the global center, the building. I think people would feel happy because it will be theirs. They would build it and they would manage it, and because it was all done by the people they'd say, "Hey, I'm going there!" The last part of my model includes the words, *The past, the present, the future and sharing.* I'd like to think that if we did get to the stage of having this wonderful center, that non-Aboriginal people would come to it too, and they could learn and help in the reconciliation process. The bottom line is that we all live in this one country and therefore we have to learn to share, but it needs to be a two-way process.

That's my dream.

Gail on the Possibilities of Actualizing the Dream

There were some trial centers. One community that I was involved with had one, but like all things when someone who is really committed leaves it doesn't necessarily continue. So, it stopped. But, eventually I know it will happen. In my lifetime I intend to see that it happens, if it's the only thing I do. I really feel strongly about it and there are lots of people who are interested. They haven't all come together, but many are all doing little bits and pieces, individual pieces. There are possibilities, I am sure of it.

The biggest barrier to making this happen would be attitudes toward Aboriginal language and its effect on funding. Some people may say,

> Why should we have this?" The education department has the LOTE department, Language Other Than English [LOTE] that takes in a huge list of languages, but there isn't actually an Aboriginal language department. We're still too White in Australia. The attitude is still, "What use is the Aboriginal language? Why do you need it? What are you going to do with it? You should be learning English.

My answer to this is that the Aboriginal language is one of the oldest languages in the world. For that reason, it needs to be preserved and maintained. Children have a right to speak their first Native language. Many children speak English, but it is still their parents' language, even though they've had to suppress it. It was my parents' language. When I was growing up, we never spoke it because we weren't allowed to. So, I didn't learn it, it is my failure not to speak it now. It's only now that I'm going back. I thought, "Wow! This is going to take forever." But I'm sticking with it although the White Australian society is very harsh. Yeah, it is. We've almost got to give a reason why we want our language and it has to be relevant to today's non-Aboriginal, society.

There are little changes that are slowly making things better; for example, the Aboriginal studies program in K–12 schools has recently been launched. Many public schools have to started to implement this curriculum, and that's very good. But, even the small language centers and the things that we do in schools can't guarantee that Aboriginal programs are going to continue year after year. If the school changes its leadership, the principal perhaps, he or she may have a different idea or focus. He or she may say, "Well, this year I want to teach Japanese." The principal has that power even if 50% of the kids are Aboriginal. I really do believe, however, that there's enough strong people who are committed to Aboriginal language and culture that will make it prosper in the future. We need to insure that it is going to happen for our young people because if we don't, we will have lost everything.

Whenever I go around the countryside to schools (I often get invited to different things because I belong to many committees as the Aboriginal Studies Association Committee for western Australia) I speak about language revitalization. If you keep talking about something, people start thinking about it, and start doing something about it. In fact, a couple schools have started language centers, and some older people are thinking about going into the schools. So you see, you just have to keep talking about it. Sometimes I just feel like saying,

> Hey everybody! What about Aboriginal people who have died for this land for forty thousand years, for God's sake! They gave us this wonderful gift of language and culture. We must have this back! Give us respect! Give us something in return for what you've taken! We're asking, can we please learn our language? Can the children have the right to learn their language?"

The old people don't want to become politically involved. They shun away from that. I suppose they're used to not standing up for themselves. As soon as one stands up for oneself and says, "Yes, I'm going to support this. This is a good idea," they'll straight away say, "Watch that one. He's an activist. Get him out of there. He's no good because he's standing up for his people, doing something." The Aboriginal people are not very aggressive. Very few are aggressive. In the justice system, there are many aborigine people who are there for fines and petty things; they shouldn't be in prison. Actually, the women are keen to start doing something in the Aboriginal language. I just mentioned it one day and they said, "Oh, we'd love to do that." And I thought, "Aha! If these women learn their Native language, they will teach it to their children!" I'm in the process of getting permission from the government to teach the Aboriginal language in the prison system. I don't know yet what will happen.

There are very few Aboriginal people who are teachers. Many of them find it difficult to fit into the school system. They have to put up with racism in the staff room and classroom; watching how negatively Aboriginal children are treated. Many of them eventually leave because the schools are still really bad. When I was working in the school, I would stand up and say something in the staff room against racism. I'd say, "I don't like that joke. I think it's racist." Some would agree and say, "Hang on, let's not have any jokes about people's race, color, whatever. If we can't tell a joke without that, then don't tell it." But, on the whole, the teachers don't care. They'd say to me, "You have to learn to walk away from it." But, for Aboriginal kids that's not easy to do. It's very hard.

I believe I have been given a job to do for my people. I feel I am on a path that has been set for me. I feel blessed and privileged to be chosen to do it, and I think I will be busy for a long time. There is work to be done.

Transition III

Path to the Spirit:
"We are walking in a sacred manner."

The themes of spirituality, love, respect for elders, and connection to our ancestors is pervasive throughout the dialogue presented in this text. Kalena Silva reminded the group that; "Our spiritual life is part of our everyday life. It is not just a ritual we do once in awhile." "In Aotearoa," Kate added, "everything begins with karakia (prayer)." Sam Suina shared that the spiritual part of all of us "serves as a means of connection to our ancestors and safeguards the way we treat one another and everything around us. We are blessed with the simplicity of our life and we find happiness with what we come across in life." Hence, the gift of life is constantly revealed in reverence and in prayer and in the knowledge that life is spiritual. This essence of spirituality is difficult to describe in written text, because it belongs to the world of oral language and dreaming. Gail Kiernan, our sister from Australia shared that, "Dreaming is not like the ordinary day dreaming or dreaming at night. To the Australian Aborigine, dreaming is reality itself! We dream the land, the mountain, the breezes because we believe it holds what is sacred given to us from the creator."

Spirituality is also contested terrain. For example, in a group discussion about spirituality, Darrell challenged the group to think more deeply about the effects of organized religion: "Religion of conformity, Western religion. We haven't said anything about it yet. I believe because we are suspicious of organized religion and because of this we embrace traditional ways more and more." Kalena reminded us that because many Native groups in North America and across the Pacific had been exposed to variations of Christianity over time, some Natives were currently more orthodox in their Christian beliefs than others. For many Native groups, Kalena observed, returning to more traditional practices, and in some cases integrating these beliefs and practices with Christian dogma, has become a trend. Listening intensely to the conversation, Sam wanted the group to remember that although many Native people have embraced other organized religions, we should not shun or disregard them. In the end, Sam shared that he believed that the current movement to "practice more traditional religious arts reveals an awareness that there is a well-spring of knowledge in our ancestors."

In essence, we all understood that to live in the absence of the sacred would mean the success of "the White man to rid us of our sun dances and would make everything we cherish disposable and for sale" (Darrell). An example of the importance of spirituality as the core of life, was shared in a journal entry by Maenette, one of the facilitators:

> Everything that I have learned about spirituality has been taught by my kūpuna (elders). I remember my grandma telling me to be careful about what I said, because the words I used were powerful in different ways. She asked me, when I was 8 years old, what I thought the meaning of "Aloha" was and I said smartly, "Hello, Good-bye, I love you." She smiled and walked away, and I thought I was pretty brilliant! Over the many years since then I have come to know that on one level "Aloha" can be simply a greeting. Yet, it has more symbolic meaning in that it embraces all that is good and that is expressed by love. My grandma had aloha for me, which shows through her genuine caring for my well being, but my grandma is the embodiment of aloha, of a way of being loving and gentle. Much deeper than this, "Aloha" is spiritual. "Alo" means to embrace and "ha" is life giving breath. Hence, "Aloha" is to walk in the embrace of life giving breath.

We were reminded of the significance of spirituality during our morning hike to the homeland of the Cochiti Pueblo. Miranda Wright wrote about this experience, "Just as we had taxed our mental resources yesterday, today we tapped our physical and spiritual self. In two days, we found common ground." Our Cochiti Pueblo host, Sam Suina, invited the participants of the gathering and called us "my Native brothers and sisters," to journey with him to a sacred place of his people. This meant a hike up a mountain to the home of his ancestors. Although many participants were excited about sharing this significant event, there was some anxiety. Rosalie Medcraft, one of the eldest in the group shared privately this concern, "My spirit is willing, but I don't know if the body is." The morning was cool, the sun warm, and the mountain much steeper than we had anticipated. Paul Johnson wrote about the climb in his journal:

> In my experiences, the access to these sites is usually difficult in the physical sense. These places are usually located in remote areas and involve a long walk or climb. I believe these physical challenges are put forth to weaken the body in order that other psychological forces might come to the front of the growth experience. To me, it's like a person that loses the gift of sight and then learns to depend on their gift of hearing to survive in their environment.

The difficulty of the climb challenged our individual physical capacities, however, as Paul suggested, it freed our spirits. Genny Gollnick shared in her journal writings the physical and spiritual importance of the hike:

> This day was incredible. I have been on hikes like this before, and I have always found myself to be short-winded. The elevation was 12,000 feet! I had to stop frequently because of my breath and heart pounding too hard. What remained the same, as other times I've climbed mountains, is my determination to get there and knowing that my travel would be different than most of the others. My heart and spirit were challenged and I felt valiant. My friends here were concerned about me, and I appreciated that. During this time I pulled into myself calling up my spirituality. I also joined forces with new friends.

Gail Kiernan also shared her physical and spiritual awakening:

> This morning I wondered what the mountain would look like. How would I feel at this special place? I was feeling very humble to be invited and to join in with my sisters and brothers in this journey that I will long remember all the days of my life. The journey was long, hard and often quite difficult. At one stage, I thought I would have to turn back. That is when I challenged myself. I said, if my brothers and sisters can do this, so can I. As I walked along, I wondered if my ancestors from my homeland were looking down on me. I also thanked Sam's ancestors for allowing me to come to this special place. We were three quarters of the way there and I was feeling very hot when all of a sudden a cool breeze came over me from below the mountain. Then I saw the most beautiful gold and black butterfly flutter past me. I knew at that moment that I was going to get to this special place and return home to tell

about it. As we came up on the flat area, we saw two hawks, which were a sign, Sam, said, that his ancestors were present.

During and after the hike, everyone celebrated the sharing, collaboration, support, and care for one another over each rocky and slippery foothold. Paul wrote, "I was amazed that none of our members quit or were deterred from reaching the top of Cochiti Mesa. The cooperative character of the group made sure that all members of our group were supported. Everyone had a role in the trip and we were successful in completing our goal." No one had realized, until after the hike, that Rosalie had not been able to physically walk up hills, let alone climb mountains. Rosalie wrote, "I wasn't going to miss it! Today's journey was meant to be. If we had not been all together here in Santa Fe, we could not have climbed to the top. We did it with the help of one another. It was a united journey, a learning and spiritual journey."

The purpose of the hike was two-fold, first, to develop deeper cooperation among participants, and second, and more important, to honor the ancestors of the land we were visiting. This genuine show of respect and honor is important for Native people as it affirms a spirituality of connectedness to the wisdom and lives of past generations. As Sam eloquently stated when conducting a spiritual ceremony in his ancestors' *kiva*, "We are walking in a sacred manner!" Miranda reflected on the significance of our hike in her journal:

> I was unsure of the purpose of our hike other than to accept the invitation of a fellow participant to visit his homeland. The invitation was graciously accepted and I looked forward to the trip. It wasn't until we arrived at the base of the Mesa that I learned we were going to the ancient ruins of a Cochiti Kiva or ceremonial center. This former settlement of the Cochiti people was abandoned in the 1500s. The significance of the journey, and the fact that a group of virtual strangers from around the world were invited, admitted, and permitted to such a sacred place, humbles me. I am honored to be treated with such trust and respect by a stranger. The ground work which we laid the previous day came together as we ascended the mesa. Together we shared the challenges of climbing in high altitude, in a hot, dry desert. Together we shared the beauty of the surrounding environment, the haunting sounds of ancient songs and stories of the spirit helpers who joined us and guided us up the path.

The ceremony in the *kiva* was respectful of Cochiti Pueblo ancestors and the land of their spirit. We do not share the ceremony in this text, because ceremonies like this are not written or described outside of that moment in time, however, one final reflection from a participant exemplifies the significance of the journey to our thinking and work in education. Jeannette wrote:

> The climb was not going to be hard if we went slowly, if we helped one another, if we didn't leave any behind. It became apparent how the physical reality and the natural world must always be the abstract, intellectual formulations and compilations of information common to Western education. That it must be about people following a path working together, the helpers and storytellers, and the teachers and the path finders and the rear guard all giving their part equally and always being aware of the blessings and messages from our spirit relatives. Remembering that the old places are still powerful and alive with sacredness, and so with our language and traditions, that all we need to do is to go to them and feed and feast. We can't see every bend in the path, even where to go next. Yet, we know a sacred place awaits and surely if we trust those who walked the path ahead then we will arrive to that sacred center at the summit of our ascent and there we will rest and rejoice.

After our morning hike, we needed time to rest and to reflect silently on the nature of the experience. Darrell wrote of the effect of the hike in his journal:

> Afternoon is arriving slowly at the lodge. The trip up the mountainside with strong sun reminds me that in a few days our OKAN begins and sunshine, powerful sunshine, pours over me and cleanses me. I don't want to change my clothes once back because the smell of sacred places resembles the smell on my shirt. I wish I could work—exhaustion renders me one with myself."

'Eiwa (Chapter 9)

Linking Native People Around the Spirituality of All Life: *"The gifts of our grandmothers and grandfathers."*

Sam Suina
Cochiti Pueblo Educator

Prologue

Although each of the models present unique visions of and for Native education particular to specific linguistic and cultural traditions, there are several common themes. In this chapter, Sam Suina's words reveal a philosophy that is replicated across other models in this volume, that the foundation of learning must be built on spirituality and wisdom shared through our Native language and traditions. The core of spirituality that is represented in our model, Go to the Source, has it's roots in Sam's model, where he defines spirituality as a connection to the beauty and strength of the earth and to the beings that inhabit her, and to the teachings of our grandparents. Connection is a key principle of the model because it fosters responsibility, constructive interrelations between individuals and groups, and respect for Native language and cultural values. In essence, spirituality connects us to our ancestors, families, friends, and homeland.

The spiritual songs and stories, that Sam shared with the group throughout our gathering encouraged educational leaders to renew and revitalize their bonds with the earth, their ancestors, the elders, and the children in their communities. What is missing in formal school situations, Suina argued, is the understanding that we are all connected, and therefore, we are all responsible for one another. Often, he observed, we don't take the time to listen and to see the special gifts that each person brings to the learning environment. Additionally, K–12 schools do not take the time to partner with other institutions (e.g., after-school programs, higher education, senior citizen groups, health organizations, etc.) to build healthy communities. Sam concluded that being driven by time (i.e., allowing our decision processes to be hurried by deadlines) has invaded our Native ways of learning, and of addressing problems, thereby creating disconnectedness and dysfunction in our families and schools.

The symbols in Sam's model are powerful reminders of the richness and depth of Native thought. He links ways of knowing and pedagogy to the sacredness of colors, to directions (north, south, east, west), seasons, and the fruits (e.g., corn, buffalo) of the earth. At its core is the storyteller, the grandmother that connects Native people to language, cultural traditions, and ceremony. Sam takes the reader an important step further, linking his philosophical lens to the practical work of schooling. He lists eight education goals that emerge from his model and presents examples of how these goals can be met through decision-making and communication skills.

Sam Suina

Sam Suina's *Linking Native People Around the Spirituality of All Life.*

The kind of model for education that I feel would be meaningful for our people, indigenous peoples, is one that would be uniquely connected to our beliefs, values, practices, and traditions. The model will simply reflect the cultural and linguistic richness of the character of the people. The overriding purpose of education would be, therefore, to help strengthen and revitalize those gifts of languages and ceremonies that were given to us by our grandmothers and grandfathers. What I've done in this model is to illustrate what it might look like for one group, the Cochiti Pueblo.

In this model, I've depicted different symbols, directions, life forms, and seasons in a circular fashion, to represent the interconnectedness and sacredness of all life and life forces. This model was designed to have special spiritual significance for Pueblo people, and is based on the kind of worldview that we, as Pueblo people, have of life.

At the heart of this model is the corn. Corn is what continues to sustain our people. In our prayers, we use corn pollen and corn meal to communicate with our grandmothers' and grandfathers' spirits. I have also included the animals, plants, and feathers in different positions to correlate with the four directions and seasons. The figures of animals, plants, feathers, rain, clouds, lightening, and sun are symbols that show the interrelatedness of all life. In the middle of the model, I placed the storyteller, who is the educator. The people of Cochiti are especially known for their many storytellers. The storyteller is always a grandmother or a mother who carries little children all over her. During the storytelling she not only engages in teaching but also in the nurturing of little ones. The grandmother, therefore, represents the teacher of our language and traditions.

I also wanted to depict the special colors that we have for our people. The yellow I used in the north is like the yellow corn, the blue corn is for the west, the red is for the south, and the white is for the east. We believe that the year begins in the winter to the north. This is a time of renewed spirit for everyone and represents the beginning of many other ceremonial traditions that will be fulfilled throughout the year. As with many other indigenous groups, we have a calendar of ceremonial events that we fulfill each year. As we start the year, new tribal officers are appointed to help in the fulfillment of those ceremonies. In the model, the buffalo represent the gift of animals and birds. At the time of the new year, we have buffalo dances, deer dances, eagle dances, and many other dances to show reverence.

As we enter spring, we begin our ceremonies for the planting season. During this season, the dances and songs relate more to the plants, clouds, lightning, thunder, rainbow, and rain. For example, during this time we have corn dances. All of these forces in life have special names and significance to our people. It is important for everyone to learn the meanings of the various dances and songs.

There's a period when it is quiet. Everything stops. For example, council meetings will stop for almost a month and a half before January. Our people believe that there are times when we need to be quiet, so ceremonies, meetings, any conflicts that arise, and generally all our business operations with the tribal government stops. This goes on for a month and a half. The people are aware of this time. So, whatever there is to take care of, our people generally make the preparations long before we enter that quiet time period.

In regard to changes that have occurred, in particular, to the legacy of assimilation and how it's impacted our cultures, I believe that we need to define our education from our value system and traditional practices. Our beliefs are what have validated us as a community for many years. The arrows on my model point in different directions. This is a symbol for how our beliefs need to spread outward to others. As we go through different ceremonies, for example, we're asking for blessings, not just for our community, but for brothers and sisters that live all over the world. We think about how our ceremony will benefit us, our loved ones, our friends, our brothers, our sisters, and those that we may not know. There's that strong inner connectedness of all life that's represented through plants, animals, the forces in life, and especially, people.

Although we have different dances, different names for our tribes, and different songs, we have a strong interconnectedness. Take, for example, the buffalo dance. The buffalo songs and dances all represent a kind of spiritual journey. We all share in this. Also, as we end many of our dances, we send our prayers to all the tribes, the indigenous people throughout the world. The arrows in my model also represent the support we offer one another in our efforts. We're all in this world to contribute to the well-being of all people. I think that these values of interconnectedness and responsibility need to be taught to our children. I think we can do that through our ceremonies and our dances. I also think that teaching these values in a natural setting, outdoors, is important.

For me, the philosophy of education is about how we build an educational foundation that recognizes the spirituality of all life. My model then is also built on the oral traditions of my people. Words are powerful. The words in our songs are powerful. Educational experiences must encourage people to speak, to learn the words together. You might think that it is easier to write down the words or record them. Then, some time later, you can pull it out and say, "Here's the song." I think there is a stronger spiritual connection when we say that we won't write it down but that we're going to all help one another to remember this song orally. We don't write it down. We believe that the song is right there when it's time to sing. I don't think there is any other way that one can recognize the deep spirituality that is linked to our words.

Our people believe that people have different gifts. Some are really good teachers and can communicate certain things well. Others are excellent composers of songs, and that is their gift. Others might be artists, and so forth. But, we all have the capacity to speak and to learn the meanings of the stories and songs. Through the oral tradition, I believe that our people have long recognized the importance of being able to relate to one another on a one-to-one basis. If you really want to learn and do things right, then you have to do things in the way where the little ones will want to be there with you. That's where the storyteller and the grandmother become important to the learning process.

There probably would not have been an effort to teach the Cochiti language, but because of circumstances that we're faced with in many of our public communities, and in Cochiti particularly, our young ones have not learned their mother language. So, Cochiti, I believe, has become a leader in this whole effort. Our small children are in classrooms, like head start, and in outdoor settings where the teaching of Cochiti is occurring. Teaching is done by our respected community members, many of whom hold special positions in the community. The people who teach the courses make a real commitment. When we enter our classrooms and ceremonies we say, "Remember what we want to do is talk Cochiti here." We've got to. If we don't, you know, the English language, it's really powerful. What used to happen, is that when an English speaker joined a group of us who were talking in our Native language, we immediately transferred to English to accommodate the non-Native speaker. We can't afford to accommodate anymore. The children are also telling us, "Teach us. We want to learn." Everyone in the community sees themselves as learners, even the ones that are the most fluent speakers can learn from a child. For example, sometimes my little one will remind me at the dinner table that we're speaking English. "Talk to us in Cochiti," he says. And so, in that sense, my little one has become a teacher reminding me of how I should function at the dinner table.

The other thing that I want to mention is that in partnerships, we need to ask Indian people working in colleges and universities to begin thinking about how they could serve in an advocacy capacity for their people. At Cochiti, if we're going to have certain learning occur, we want to structure it so it comes from us, and not the dominant institution. For example, we can bring our youth leadership group from Cochiti to the challenge course at Santa Fe Community College. We can use the ropes course and different exercises to teach not only Cochiti words but also Cochiti concepts. The college doesn't structure the learning, we do. Someday, we hope to structure more learning places so that everything is more in the natural environment, like in a ceremonial house and a den.

What I have learned from my years at Penn State University and from many years working with my community, is that any philosophy of education for indigenous people must be rooted in spirituality and in the oneness of all indigenous people. I believe that there are eight educational goals that can help us build healthy communities and raise healthy children. These goals are as follows:

1. Support networking among indigenous people across the globe.
2. Support efforts that strengthen communities by inclusiveness and validating members.
3. Support language, traditions, and values from a tribal perspective.
4. Support and validate pride among our young people and to support tribal names of people.
5. Support collaborative partnerships.
6. Focus on experiential learning.
7. Develop teaching practices that follow traditional methods and develop evaluation processes that are nonjudgmental.
8. Maintain self-determination as the ultimate goal.

There are ways that I think we can begin our work, but we must first begin with dialogue. The way we communicate with one another and create the context for dialogue is critical. When we have committee meetings, it is always important to start out with a blessing, which connects us to our traditions and practices that are gifts to us from our grandmothers and grandfathers. This connects us not only to our ancestors, but also to our grandchildren. Whatever we do, the dialogue must be respectful. We also understand that we are together for the children and not for ourselves, and that our work is about finding some outcome that represents the collective good of the people.

Creating respectful dialogue also helps us with decision making. When we begin to make decisions about a particular topic or activity we may want to pursue, the questions that is usually asked is, "How do you feel about this as individuals?" Everyone has an opportunity to talk and to question. As we talk and ask questions, clarifying our perceptions and perspectives, we collectively begin to come to a conclusion. When we reach a conclusion, we then ask, "Is this good with all of you?" If it is not, we talk more. It is then we move on. I think the way we make decisions is also a good educational practice.

I believe that the best educational practices are ones that reflect true inclusion of people in making decisions. These situations validate the way we communicate with one another, and at the same time, instill the value of respect for one another. In the classroom, with little children, we must allow them to be open and free in their responses. We need to first call them by their Indian names. This is a real validation because they hear that they are not "John," but that in this Native environment they are Native children.

Then, when we ask questions, we allow them to answer in the best way that they can. Instead of saying, "No, you're wrong." You respond respectfully with, "Good! Here's another way to say that." I also believe that laughter is critical in teaching.

This is the way we talk respectfully to one another and are inclusive. It is important to embrace our Native brothers and sisters. We hear so often how our people, once they leave their Native communities, have a difficult time returning home because they feel ostracized by their own people. I was welcomed back to my community. My time away was irrelevant. They respected whatever learning experiences I had outside of my community. They trusted me. The message to me has always been, "You're here for your people. You're here for the children. You're here for the community." I believe this is a message that needs to be sent by tribal elders to the many Native youth who go to mainstream colleges and universities.

This time working with the other participants and sharing and building our models has truly been wonderful for me. I cannot recollect a time outside of my own community where I felt so spiritually connected. It has taught and reaffirmed for me the need to work collectively with indigenous people throughout the world. We have learned and shared messages that inspire! We learn to move forward in a manner that validates the dreams and hope of our grandmothers and grandfathers' spirits. We are reminded that we must remain focused on service to our children. Through networking, I believe that language initiatives can grow. I believe that collectively, we can strengthen holistic education and revitalize efforts that validate the sacredness of life, of people, and of our Native languages.

'Umi (Chapter 10)

Creating a Ceremony: "Nature's Model from the Longhouse People."

Genevieve Gollnick
Oneida Educator

Prologue

Genevieve begins her presentation by sharing a creation story linking her home, Turtle Island, and her people, the Oneida, to Sky Woman. She continues to discuss education by weaving the traditional values of On ^ yo?te.aka (the people of the Standing Stone, Oneida) with the pressures and situations of the modern day world. The tensions created by the collision of the traditional and the contemporary, she explains, can be understood, and effectively addressed, by Oneida youth who have the tools of a strong cultural value system and the skills to navigate in an increasingly global and technological society. She explains that the starting point for this work is to change negative stereotypes about Native Americans that tend to create barriers for Oneida youth.

Genevieve's vision for learning begins with teaching students the prayers and rituals that give meaning and belonging to all Oneida people. This, she explains, creates pride and control of life choices, that are powerful tools that lead to the dismantling of the colonized mind and to self and community sovereignty. Her model highlights the importance of spiritual gifts that include love and faith, sharing and gaining knowledge, the importance of giving thanks for good health and well-being, and the necessity to teach Native language, history, and cultural tradi-

tions. In addition, her model, from the Longhouse people, not only adds value and meaning to the Go to the Source model, but also translates its conceptual principles to practice. Genevieve introduces her current initiatives that include the development of an Oneida Teacher Certification program, designing professional development opportunities for non-Native teachers in Oneida culture and language, and projects to link educators and Native leaders in an effort to integrate language and culture into the curriculum and pedagogy at Turtle School.

The Turtle School at Onieda is a unique, tribally developed BIA grant school that promotes community and cultural values. The teachers, administrators, and community members have worked hard to incorporate Oneida life ways into the environment, structure, and ways of learning and teaching at the school. For example, the ideal that everyone is equal and that all are learners and teachers are fundamental to the practice of schooling. Because teachers see themselves as facilitators, they work to challenge individual students and provide them with the tools and time each student needs to develop their skills. At the same time, a fundamental principle of the school is that the students are challenged continually and trained to be responsible for their learning. A feature of this pedagogy is that because it builds self-esteem and the motivation for learning, the dialogue in the classes presses students to think more critically about current social issues and problems their people face. What they begin to learn is that there are many ways to view a problem and more than one way to address it. Critical, creative, and responsible thinking are the fruits of the Oneida school philosophy. This educational goal is essential to all the models presented in this volume.

Genevieve Gollnick

Genevieve Gollnick's Creating a Memory.

I feel honored to be able to share an educational model from nature. The interpretation displayed in the model is obtained from the Longhouse people who live in the northeast. The pictorial impression comes from the teachings of the *Peacemaker*. The Peacemaker founded the *Houdinosaunee* (Longhouse), or, *Six Nations League*. The belief system of the Longhouse uses the universal laws of the environment to mold and support government and community values. As knowledge grows from the message of peace, its purity and power transcend our humanity.

From the art materials laid out on the table, I have made a design for the purpose of this presentation. The image depicts the world that existed before this world. The earth was dark and covered by water when Sky Woman, who was pregnant, entered it. The cord (which is silver) on the picture connects the first world with this one. All teachings flow from the celestial world down the cord. The things that are part of creation here have come from the first world. Sky Woman became the first person to live in this world. She brought life and hope for the future. When she fell through a hole in the sky, birds caught her and put her on the back of the turtle. The

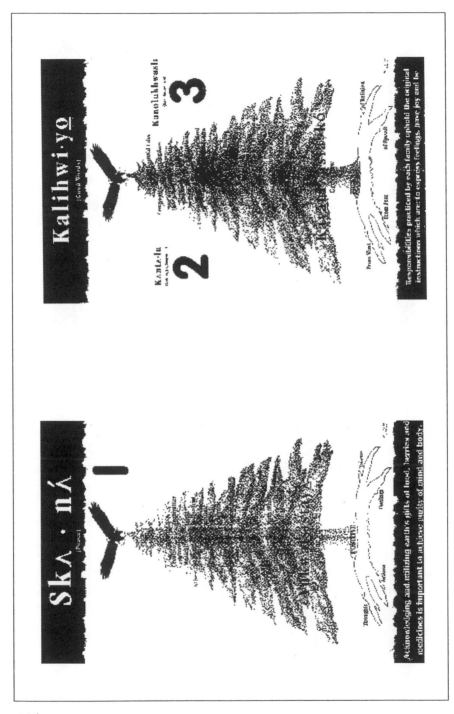

Sk∧·ná
[Peace]

1

Acknowledging and utilizing earth's gifts of food, berries and medicines is important to achieve purity of mind and body.

Kalihwi·yo
[Good Words]

Ka·te·lu
[to Advocate?]

2

Kanolukhwaslʌ
[to love out]

3

Responsibilities practiced by each family uphold the original instructions which are: to express feelings, love joy and be

104

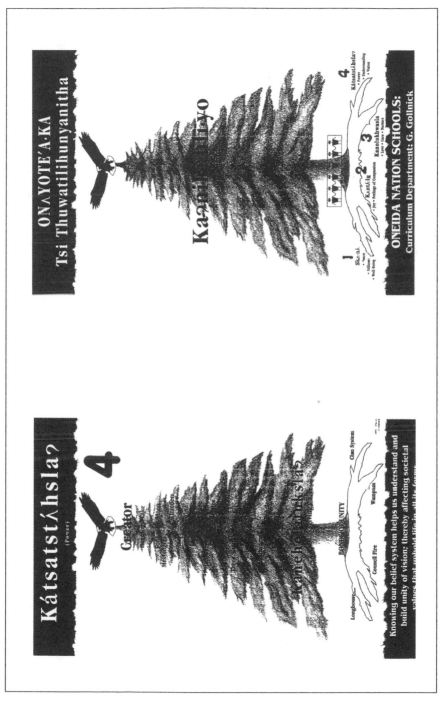

ONʌYOTEʔAꞏKA
Tsi Thuwatilihunyanitha

Kaʔ... ...Tyo

ONEIDA NATION SCHOOLS:
Curriculum Department: G. Gollnick

1 Sk... ...ʌ
• Peace
• Stillness
• Well-Being

2 Kaʌt... ...ʌ
• Joy
• Feelings of Compassion

3 Kanolúkhwasla
• Love
• Care
• Nurture

4 Kátsatstʌ́hsla ?
• Power
• Understanding
• Vision

Kátsatstʌ́hsla ?
(Power)

4

Creator

Kemeh... ...aotukslaʔ

BOND OF UNITY

Longhouse   Council Fire   Wampum   Clan System

Knowing our belief system helps us understand and
build unity of vision; thereby affecting societal
values that uphold life in all its forms.

105

turtle is the image for North America. This is why we refer to North America as *Turtle Island*. On my design, I placed feathers with contrasting spots. The contrast is significant, as it represents the tension of moving from night to day and back again. When it is night, the stars brilliantly burst with beauty and meaning. Grandmother Moon enters on a cyclical basis, thus, assuring earth's balance. At twilight, the balance between day and night is heralded by the morning and evening star. This life cycle transition, from spring to fall and fall to spring, is announced through the falling and rising of *Pleiades*. The tension is life's creative properties bringing about change and constant movement. Tension occurs through the ebb and flow of the *polarities*. The polarities are the earth's magnetic fields, male and female, acid and alkaline, summer and winter, night and day, active and passive, and so on.

As an educator, I am gaining courage. Through prayer and ritual, I am seeking clarity to achieve the spiritual gifts of knowledge, peace, love, and faith. I am learning about the people around me and their spiritual gifts. My role is to peel away the definitions that hold Native children back. By definitions I refer to stereotypes and misunderstandings about who they are as Native children. It is important to let all children know they are beautiful, and that collectively, they can help each other succeed. There is a story that an author–friend, Gretchen Mayo, and I have been co-writing that we have titled, *The Trouble with Acorns*. Our intent is to bring an appreciation for the cultural worldview of Native people.

> Elder Brother Sun had journeyed all the way to the top of the sky dome before Squirrel's neighbor, Frog, poked his head out of the pond at the edge of the forest. Blink-blink. Frog looked around with his big, round eyes. Good! No one else was there! Frog leaped onto the shore. He jump-jumped away and vanished into the pines. In a blink, Frog was back, but he was not jumping this time. Fump-fump-fump. Frog crept like a turtle. He shoved one, two, three, four red acorns under a rock. Then he carefully patted soft moss over this hiding place. Looking very pleased with himself, Frog sang a long, low, jug-a-rum out over the pond.

> The Celestial Bear shone brightly over the pine forest. Squirrel had settled down to sleep in a tall pine. Out on the pond, Frog was singing to Grandmother Moon. Woodchuck climbed out of his burrow and went right to work digging a fresh hole in the ground. Scrape, scrape. What a lot of work! Suddenly, Woodchuck jumped out of the hole and ran into the pines. In a flash, he returned with bulging cheeks. Woodchuck looked up, down, and around. Then he dropped one, two, three red acorns into the hole. Woodchuck worked until Elder Brother Sun returned to the sky. Then, he covered his hole with tufts of grass and settled down to sleep away the new day.

Like other cultural messages, this story passes on a teaching to Oneida children through the tradition of the spoken word. The speaker can choose to emphasize different aspects of the story to address a particular issue or to entertain an audience. The speaker (or in this case the writers) synthesize information and actively create in the moment. The oral tradition of the storyteller thrives as an inductive process. Conversely, there is an oral tradition that exists where the communication process is passive. The speaker is meant to be a recorder of the spoken word. The speaker, known as the *runner*, may attend a meeting representing leaders who are not present. The runner listens and observes, making careful analysis of what is happening. He returns home and is expected to repeat, without error, the words he heard (formal and informal) that were said in the meetings. In order for problem solving to have meaning and quality, accurate information is of critical importance. The runner knows his role and keeps it. In the oral tradition, the runner's role as the channel in the communication process is deductive.

There are multiple levels of learning for children and youth that address physical and emotional health. Socially, team building and cooperation is encouraged. There is the intellectual, thinking side, that needs development. There are many tensions that challenge our youth, so we need to develop resources that are helpful. At our school, we are striving to build our traditional stories into the academics. As an organization, we are coming closer to our goals of helping the students with both cultural and academic–technical resources. The intent is to ensure that our students may more confidently work through multiple steps and complete complex tasks.

The Oneida Nation school system is based on Longhouse teachings, that include the life cycle ceremonies, the Great Peace (or the constitution of the Five Nations), and *Kaiwi-yo* (Good Words). This is the label that refers to the teachings that were received by Handsome Lake through visions and prophecies. These teachings incorporate the principles and laws that have existed since the beginning of time. Structurally, the school is constructed in the shape of a turtle. In the center of the turtle's back there is a glass dome on the roof that represents the hole in the Creator's world where Sky Woman fell through. The school has the creation story laser-etched in the interior corridor. There are purple and white tile belts on the outside of the school walls that depict our most important laws. Our school philosophy is comprised of the teachings that the spiritual leaders, chiefs and clan mothers have inculcated. We have a phrase, *Coming of one mind.* Thinking the same way with the same effort can be instrumental in helping other things

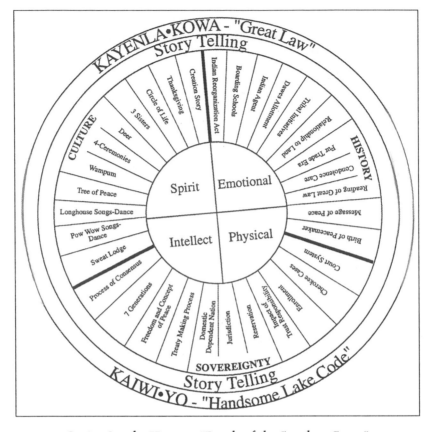

On ^ yo?te.aka Heritage "People of the Standing Stone"

in the world. Consensus is an ultimate goal for communication. It includes multiple perspectives and gaining knowledge. Reaching consensus means attaining success.

There are four posters (they appear on pages 104 and 105 in this chapter) in our school, that reflect the teaching of Peacemaker and are also designed to represent the cultural curriculum of *tsi? Thuwatilihunya.nita* (Oneida Nation Schools; Where they teach the People of the Standing Stone). The posters were developed by me to help connect an ancient message of Peace, Power, and Righteousness to today's world. Through my friendship with many people, my knowledge has grown. I would like to thank Bob Brown (Oneida Chief, Confederacy), Marian Hinton and Amos Christjohn (Oneida Elders of Wisconsin), Dr. Cliff Abbott (Oneida Linguist, University of Wisconsin–Green Bay), and my husband William Gollnick (mentor and educator) for their wisdom.

The Peacemaker's message incorporates four parts. It begins with peace, stillness, and well-being. These modern day adjectives on the pine tree poster describe lifestyle and talents. The second part is joy. It is the outward expression of feelings of compassion and love and takes the form of laughter. The third part is similar to the second. It represents the acts of love, caring, and nurturing. When the Peacemaker came here, he used the white pine as a symbol for peace. He said the teachings of the great law are here in the branches. The 50 chiefs of the Five Nations together sat beneath the tree. Its four roots extend to the four directions. Anyone wanting to seek the message of peace may follow the roots to its source.

The fourth message is power. Power is exemplified through understanding, vision, and faith in the Creator. I am not speaking of power in the sense of a negative control of others, but of knowing oneself and having the confidence to fulfill a vision of peace. I look at this as faith combined with knowledge, which produces wisdom. *Bonds of unity* are the symbols used to remember our responsibility as humans. Symbols, such as the Longhouse, fire, wampum, and the clan system connect us with our belief system. We need the bonds of unity of vision, thereby affecting societal values that uphold life in all its forms. The clans also create kinship among people. We are not only relatives to other people, but our ties also go to the winged ones, the four-leggeds, and those who swim. We have strong connections to the environment and all of Mother Earth. This is basically a summary of themes of peace, which are the ancient teachings of the Longhouse people.

How do we apply these messages to the Oneida Nation schools? The four roots lay the foundation. If you look at it that way, the foundation is built on developing a healthy mind and a healthy body. We are seeing the person who is a listener, meditative and tranquil, but we are also seeing them with talents and gifts. Learning is a self-actualization process. We need to connect academic learning and social skills to rituals and ceremonies. This makes us stronger and healthier. In our model, we include gifts of food, berries, and medicines that are important to achieve purity of mind and body. We have food for sustenance. Other gifts of creation are also our sustenance, such as medicine plants, that help us emotionally and spiritually.

Another example of integrating our rituals into the academics is the Thanksgiving Address, which comes to us from the beginning of time. The address gives formal recognition to everything that exists. First, we thank the creator for making a particular item. Second, that the creator continues to carry out its "Original Instructions" from the beginning of time, thereby fulfilling its responsibility. And third, we express our appreciation and gratitude. Although we give thanks for things in the natural and spiritual worlds, we often forget to give thanks to ourselves and each other. To honor oneself and others starts the process. We are working to develop organizational habits of mind and rituals to honor each other and ensure that each is supported in the pursuit of success.

Although our school works hard to honor Oneida traditions, we have the same societal problems as every other place. It is an uphill struggle. For example, in the schools' early history we had a larger percentage of Oneida people on staff. There is a profound understanding and motivation when Oneida work with Oneida children. Yet, because the schools have grown with an additional 200 students, this growth of classrooms and professional staff has significantly changed the balance. This creates different tensions. There are a few people (non-Native) who truly come with good intentions, but because they may see through the lens of the "missionary spirit" they do not perceive that On ^ yote'a.ka (Oneida people) have something real and valid to share. Their actions might be interpreted as "patting the kids on the head." Sometimes tensions really explode. Our Native ways need to be reflected in the teacher's practice! To varying degrees we must remake our staff to exemplify the persona of the real person the community desires to be our teachers. Because I believe it is important that the teacher create the ceremony in which the children participate, I will continue to work to get more Native teachers. When I say *Native teacher* it indicates a person who is able to teach Native children credibly and authentically.

Since the mid-1990s, we have known the importance of having our own Oneida Teacher Certification (ONTC). One has been drafted and approved. An ONTC requires taking 18 credits of Oneida culture, history and language courses in 3 years. Each teacher submits an Individual Learning Plan. Although the program is still in the development stage, I have observed a difference in the quality of our teaching staff. I hope that ONTC will have a long-term, positive effect on academic learning and on socially competent human beings.

For instance, if the non-Native teachers with the missionary spirit say, "No, I am not going that far [teaching Native ways]," they may move on after 3 years. Before this happens, we hope that the teacher would take the initiative and say, "Maybe this is not the place for me." There are non-Native teachers who do want to stay and learn. We have several different ways to assist them. For one thing, they are required by their teacher contract to take a 1-hour a week language class, which an elder teaches. On Wednesday afternoons, there are required minicultural sessions that may be on any topic; such as crafts, or stories of the people. We also encourage teaching the symbols of the confederacy. It is preferable to learn the topic from a Native perspective then incorporate it into their teaching. Often, the typical teacher says, "I don't have time." I respond, "We know that it's going to take a lot of time, but there will be a lot of growth being realized." As we travel together we will meet the goals. It is important to choose a topic that brings a high interest to self and students.

Although we have many wonderful and productive things going on in our school, we do have challenges. Among the most significant is the effort to preserve our language. We have goals and ideas, but it is hard to incorporate them into a curriculum. I think we have all been challenged, including myself, to develop new curriculum and teaching models. Anywhere there is a gathering of Native people working on curriculum and teaching, I want to be there. I want to learn more, so that I can work most effectively with teachers. I want to link our traditions and language to academics and an oral–literate continuum.

Because our history of oppression has damaged many egos, there is still a lot of self- and cultural analysis that we must do to overcome these wounds. The history of oppression has created many Native American communities who produce self-inflicted wounds that can hold their community down, often through alcoholism or almost insurmountable feelings of jealousy. Unfortunately, this is an area that is not discussed openly. A friend reminds me, at these times, that the "past does not equal the future." The question becomes, "How do we reawaken souls to the beauty within?" The toughest challenge is learning to honor ourselves.

I think education for our Native American children is important because it is all about freeing the mind. I also know we can not do it alone. As Native educators we have a role in the story. I am excited because I think Native people are responding to each other and fitting their roles together. Some teachers have the analytical knowledge to teach the core academics, some people have the life experiences, some people have ceremonial knowledge, and some know how to make it all pragmatic. I look at all the teachers among us from whom we may gain insights. Thanks to my work as a curriculum director, I have the opportunity to learn so much from many Native experts. I can rejoice in new learning. What joy!

Transition IV

Path to Community
"We want to remain the person that stops and cares for the grandparent."

Throughout the gathering, the educational leaders worked diligently to define holistic approaches to Native programs by capturing, and grounding learning, goals, and processes in Native values and culture. At the core of many of our conversations were the principles of respect for elders, embracing of the extended family, and protection of children. It came as no surprise that the Native educational leaders would create models that accented community involvement in the learning and teaching process. L.A. Napier shared her belief that "Native communities must define their own educational needs and become responsible and capable of addressing those needs. Also, Native communities must begin to support one another to sustain good efforts."

In the five models that follow, we share a variety of ways that a community can rally their forces to make a difference and engage in social change. What we can learn from the models is that there must be a common purpose, and continued dialogue, to critically (and helpfully) frame these new learning initiatives. In addition, a respect for individual values and experiences is necessary to create innovative programs. Indeed, what we've learned from each model presented in this book, especially Miranda

Wright's, is the necessity to facilitate and honor every individual—from the elder to the child—in our efforts. Finally, we believe that all educational programs must be grounded in Native values. Educational leaders must ground their community work on common purpose, critical dialogue, respect for individual knowledge and experience, and Native values (those particular to their group).

An example of community action, that draws on individual values, Native knowledge, and group discussion, was experienced during our final gathering activity. The final process was to bring participants together to define a collective model. Because each person's model was an extension of their spirit, intellect, and body, we understood that a single model for Native education could not fully represent the depth, complexity, nuance, and spirit of Native education. We knew, however, that a model that captured the essence of our work together would give meaning and purpose to the important process of education. It also made sense that this community effort to develop a Native way of framing education would be presented in story form.

The individual voices of the Native leaders present at the gathering are woven together in the following collective story through the ritual of a *talking circle*, using the power of the talking stick from the lightning tree. Following is the story that was shared.

Maori Blessing of Song and Dance: Susan, Kate, and Linda.

> L.A.:   Maenette, here is our model that we give to you. We know that you will need to translate this for Native people who are not here and for non-Native people. We believe that our collective model, depicted in written form, cannot represent our ideas. Because the written form is a Western technology, we present our collective model in different voices. The substance can be found in the bodies and minds of indigenous people. We share through our oral traditions of telling and singing stories.

> Linda: In this place, at this time, these people came together from diverse communities, most traveling many miles to get here. These people came from different points of the earth to answer a call issued by one of us, but some believe that this call came from a place far beyond. We were strangers at first, harboring vague notions of the task ahead and unsure of what realities we would share. There came among us a person of this place [Sam] who soon revealed to us his powerful beliefs and faith in his people and how his cultural beliefs and practices were woven into the practice of his life.

He took us on a learning journey by inviting us to a special place. The journey was difficult and we faced many hazards, which we worked through together overcoming each barrier on our way to achieving our goal. Now, we know in our hearts that this journey revealed important lessons about our reality. Learning is a journey beset equally by joy and danger, but a leader can guide us on the journey by providing a foundation of physical, spiritual, intellectual and cultural resources which offer security and safety while encouraging us to take risks necessary to achieve our goal. This journey becomes the framework for the individuals of this group to weave their own stories. Each individual will now pick up the thread left by the last speaker and weave their story of their journey. The energy, power contained within this piece of the lightning tree will fortify them and keep them to their true path.

Darrell: I thought of the notion of many thousands of years passing being a very short time, and extending ourselves out beyond our own standing by whatever means possible to extend ourselves to that ascent. The ascent was important, because I went from thinking it was a mere trip, to putting a lot of emphasis on every moment of this time. The analogy is so powerful that I can continue to extend it as long as I want. The notion of problem-solving when talking of a model; many problems are in front of me that had no solution. I always maintained that the answer would become apparent to me. Yesterday and today, and when I leave to go home from here, the process will continue as long as I can remember the time here.

Jeannette: When I started on the journey and stood in the circle before the climb, when Sam talked about the place and where we were going and the power of place and telling about feeling the spirit, I was thinking to myself. The way I like to view things I always sort of cleared the trails. Always in the front. For this ascent, I wanted to be at the end, to watch how others were doing. I really wanted to think about things I have been doing in education because if enough people are inspired to do the work, we can find the trail and see what needs to be done. To see the way. There's something I need to do from where I am and it is to observe the way of the process and what might be left behind to pick up so no one is left behind. This is a different position for me.

Another thing, when we start, we jump in and go and get so caught up we don't think of the realities of others. Others may not be able to make that ascent. I want to think of that. It is very important. The trip gave me that perspective which is a part of the model.

One other thing, I had no hat, so I borrowed some money and Genny got a hat for me that said Santa Fe, and the bill of the hat was red. This is definitely not something I would normally buy because in our tradition unless someone is a medicine person you wouldn't wear the red. I would not have chosen the red bill. Genny wouldn't know that. While we were standing in circle I put it on and it attracted the hummingbird. It was a shock. The hummingbird brings a message in our tradition. The hummingbird came back to me all the way through the hike. The hummingbird does a really significant thing; it draws the nourishment from the flower and makes something magic. It is a magnificent thing to draw sweetness and create energy. Sweetness to me is the beauty of what we ingest, and enjoy, and crave. Sweetness is that part which needs to be drawn from each individual and must be included in the model. Those specific small things I picked up. The journey is a significant model to use.

Genny: The hummingbird was there until we started down the trail. It sounded like bells, light bells. I am thinking of the adventure. I have trouble with climbing mountains, but I believed that there was meaning to the struggle and that there would be something I would learn. I didn't know what, but I knew it would be a spiritual event for all of us together. The hardest part was to get there. It took me a long time because of the thin air. I had to stop to catch my breath. Someone asked me, at one point, if I was all right. Most times I feel bad because I hold people back. What was different for me climbing this mountain was the group. Somebody always stayed back with me, but it didn't make me feel like a burden [tears]. This is different and I really appreciated it.

What was important was getting there. Being there was so incredible with Sam as our teacher. I connected with my elders' teachings. I have my own thinking about group bonding and momentum. I tried to add momentum to the energy and that was worth every minute. Something to carry forth as a memory and to share in the future. The mountain is a significant universal symbol, a model.

Sarah: We will never be alone again. To get to Cochiti Mesa, the goal, we needed to take many steps. We struggled with individual issues, but we arrived and that made people come together. During yesterday's climb to the *kiva* we saw vast areas. We can take and adapt what we experienced. The hike was like our own educational journey. We stopped to take breathers and watch what was around us. In our model, we all need to work together in order to achieve a goal. In any struggle, we need to stop and be aware.

Kalena: I am lost for words. Those same things you have said, I feel. I can say a couple of things. Our work on Thursday was difficult and frustrating. Why? Because until the trek yesterday, because as good as our intentions were, we were dealing with an abstract idea of what the model should be.

However, the trek to the *kiva* provided us with the physical and spiritual pieces that enhanced the intellectual and revealed to us the way our model should be. I also think we were hindered because we did not know each other's cultures and did not feel too comfortable. Until Friday morning, there were no shared experiences as a community, and we know that a common experience helps us move forward. I wasn't sure what we would find at the top of the mountain. Would it seem dead, old, no life there because it had not been occupied since the 1500s? Such a long time. The spirit of ancestors. I knew they were there. There seemed to be something about the butterfly. Sam, you knew the butterfly came from the north. With that observation, all of us began to observe and understand the world around us. We could begin to make sense of what we saw. The butterfly kept going around. Then there was thunder. You [Sam] said that was the grandfathers' spirit. You [Sam] began to help us see it was a living place, not dead at all. The second thing, in the *kiva*, honoring ancestors is a part of your culture, also. Spiritual values are part of a worldview. In Hawai'i today, people feel the missionaries have done too many bad things, have changed value systems, and that our own *mana* has diminished. We have become angry and rebellious. Many in Hawai'i are trying to forsake Christianity and embrace the old gods. To me this dishonors our ancestors. When you [Sam] said that, it really resonated for me.

Paul: It never fails to amaze me what happens in those places [*kiva*] that are difficult to get to. It is difficult for me to get to these ceremonies because of time and what I have to do to get there. I dialogue with myself: "Do I need to be there or here?" I wondered what I would do on this hike, because I talked about all my ailments. I need to work at getting better health. All that physical stuff didn't come into play. There was no way that if I started I wasn't going to get there. I said to myself: "Slow down." I had to constantly remind myself that when I have an idea I need to slow down and help others. I must say, "Slow down. Back up," for me, another reaffirmation that Paul needs to slow down to help the system. I found myself back with Genny. We were talking. Often, I don't take time to listen; I share with others, but I don't always listen. The trip for me was a reaffirmation of many things that I know. It came at a good point, because I am constantly in a changing state in my own life, but I am coming closer to what I need to do. It has taken longer than I thought, but the trip helped with that.

The other thing with Ojibwe today is that we talk about what we want for future generations. We talk about our elders and decisions they made. I don't want to put too much responsibility on the elders, but I want to understand why they decided what they did. We are now in the same position, and we are making decisions for future generations in many areas. We can only hope to make sound and informed decisions and keep that same set of goals in front of us. For me to go to the *kiva*, I wondered, did those elders really have in mind what was coming? We must be thankful that those sacred places exist. We must make the decisions so those after us can understand what we did.

Miranda: First I want to say, I have written models. Some things came to me about how we were all challenged to get to the top. One of the first things I felt, was the honor of land and culture to take strangers to this place. Also, the trust that was given to all to reach the place that was most powerful. The discussion we have had is about the need for love, unconditional love and trust, symbolized in our trip. When going up the mountain, we all went at our own pace, taking our time, and taking the opportunity to feel the beauty of the place. A desert, but beautiful. We stopped and prayed. When Sam saw the butterfly, I heard the story of what it meant, and I connected it with my culture. The monarch butterfly brings a message that something is about to happen. I felt curious about what might happen. A messenger might have generated the journey we were on. I felt I was recharged even with all the baggage I brought with me. Coming back over slippery rocks I learned to take my time and slow down, to stop and smell the roses, and to enjoy the people and the breeze.

Rosalie: Your mountains [referring to Sam] are mountains. I had my doubts about getting up there. I asked the tree [the tree hit by lightning Wednesday evening] for strength and wisdom. I haven't been able to walk uphill for a long time. Sam stretched the truth about sun and shade, and it was a "flat, 45-minute" hike. I think our journeys in education are just like that. We have our own ideas. I get very confused in my head, but through the journey I saw the picture so clearly. We must not forget our purpose. I had so much inspiration going up the hill. It made me realize that where I come from there are too few people who share and inspire others. It was so clear. Before I couldn't see it at all. I want to thank everybody for their love and encouragement.

Sam: [Begins in his Cochiti language.] The first thing I want to communicate to you, in my language, is to thank you from my heart, brothers, sisters, grandmothers, and grandfathers. We have loved each other and cried about each other. Second, I want to thank you all for being with us yesterday, and enjoying the chiliburgers after the hike [laughter]. For accepting the chiliburgers [laughter]. The experiences that we have had together I can only say are very blessed, a reaffirmation of who we are, our beliefs, and how we have the capacity to treat each other as brothers and sisters. That's what going to Cochiti Mesa was for me, a very blessed time of songs, prayers, and the feeling of our spirits. Just as we are happy at how things turned out, I know our grandmothers and grandfathers are happy. These are gifts from grandparents for whatever purpose we were brought together. This is a really special group. Some of you have had dreams and different experiences, which are all validations that this is good. I knew that we would go up to the mountain and walk, truly connected. I saw that. When people needed help to get up the trail or when we needed to rest, we helped each other. We looked around and communicated with one another. I do feel like a child of the land, nothing else. To me, the inspiration we gave one another is what is so sacred. I have not been with a group outside of my ceremonies where I have seen such unconditional love for one another. It enriches us, touches us.

Another thing I want to say. The stories we are sharing, it's incredible how closely our experiences have been, how significant those have been. Also the beauty, beautiful women, the knowledge, the wisdom of our people I see captured in you. I see the spirituality of people, emotion, love, compassion, also the humor, the delight in all of you. I appreciate and thank you.

Kate: [Begins in her Maori language.] We are enriched and have been enlightened. Yes, it was funny, we didn't know where we were going on the map [laughter]. It was really hot, that was all we knew, but it was one of the most beautiful places. Sam was our foundation because he led us. Some highlights of the journey were that I needed to be near to Sam to hear and listen to his teachings. I learned many lessons. The parallel I want to make is that as teachers and facilitators, had we been given a more challenging or more abstract picture, we might not have gone. We were all captured. The sun was affecting me, the air affecting my lungs. I was totally inspired by Rosalie, because she has a lot of humor. We were building a strong group complete with humility and humor, the full range. If we take children and youth on that sort of journey we've captured them. The spiritual essence at the top of the mountain is parallel to thousands of experiences in life. I was blown away by that observation. Our model will be dynamic and one built on experience.

Susan: Why do we always look outside ourselves for answers? Yesterday was an experience of learning for all of us. How did we do? We pushed ourselves physically, challenging ourselves mentally, and feeling ourselves spiritually. This is what we want a young person or child to do. To explore physically, intellectually, and spiritually. That is the essence of what we had to do yesterday. When we came to talk about how this model had to work I asked, "Why look outside of our day? Outside of the next hour of our life?" Everything has a message, an interpretation. If we can pass on this essence to children what will we have done for them? Everything.

We can look at the journey. I didn't know why we were going, but we had to be there. Each experience shows a stretch in identity. As an indigenous person, we provide deeper understanding in everything we do. It's hard to keep hold of that essence. When I got to the *kiva*, I could see our ancestors coming up with us. When I looked through the buildings, I could see my people and your [Sam's] people. When we talked about the *kiva*, the umbilical cord that is the essence of the connection of past and future, I could see and feel. I want to provide that for my children, understand, and breathe every minute of your life.

Gail: My trip from Western Australia; I wasn't sure I would come. I didn't have a ticket until Wednesday of last week and I thought if I am not meant to be there, okay. On Thursday, the travel agent rang and said the ticket had arrived. I thought, oh well, I'm meant to make this journey, but I wasn't sure. When the time drew near for our hike, I wasn't sure I could make it, but I said yes, I will do it. I will deal with the issues when they happen. When Sam said we're going up there to that flat space I looked at everybody else. It was the support of everyone that got me up there. Supporting one another was my safety net and that's what this gathering has been like. We're all in this even though we go our different ways tomorrow. We are forever linked. This is the foundation of our framework.

L.A.:   I think it is time to go now. We have said what we have needed to say and now it is time to take it back into our own context.

In the end, we realized that contemporary (often non-Native) writers have been keen to romanticize the Native ways (employing Native rituals in their principles of leadership and organization), often giving the impression that the indigenous people have all the answers. Our story and our model is certainly not the answer for all but one of many stories that can offer lessons. We would never be presumptuous to infer that our answer was for everyone. We had come to understand during our gathering that the answers we sought, as Native people, to our own dilemmas could be found in our language and culture. For this reason, we believe that we are all on a journey to seek answers to the challenges that we must face as marginalized and forgotten people, and that we, all Native people, must share in this quest.

'Umi kūmākahi (Chapter 11)

Building Linkages Across the Community: "To take action, takes great courage and strength."

L.A. Napier
University of Colorado at Denver
Member Cherokee Nation, Oklahoma

Prologue

Every model in this collection places at its core the learner, reflected in the Go to the Source model. L.A.'s narrative broadens our thinking about developing strong educational centers by including, in fact advocating for, partnerships with higher education institutions and other community organizations, both public and private. L.A. Napier's professional experiences in K–12 schools and, currently, in academe present invaluable insight and understanding regarding the necessity for Native groups to reach out and invite public and private agencies to participate in educational reform efforts. However, she warns that the community, not the outside organization, must define the shape and substance of the involvement. Allowing outsiders to define needs, purposes, and strategies are far too reminiscent of colonial dominance that is still very much a part of our collective memory.

The purpose of partnerships is twofold; first, to further enhance the intellectual community of the schools through linkages with higher education institutions. As L.A. suggests, this can bring needed technical expertise and resources. Second, linkages with public and private agencies can add important services (e.g., health, social, computer technology) and funding to support innovative initiatives and school-related projects. Although partnerships add value to the learning experiences of children and youth, and to the development of school-related reform efforts they also provide schools with a unique opportunity to participate in broader community development activities.

Advocacy for partnerships and collaboration is an integral feature of this volume because it speaks to the importance of schools as the anchor that engages the community in social, cultural, and educational events and discussion that lead to community empowerment. This move toward community sovereignty is an essential first step toward building social, economic, and physical capital to support and sustain Native communities. We argue that just as the learner's family, extended family, and Native community members must be engaged in the process of learning and teaching, the school must engage community members in intentional efforts to build social, economic, cultural, and physical capital. What these partnerships look like, of course, is greatly dependent on the needs of the community. Nevertheless, partnerships are necessary. The benefits include community leadership development, introduction of technical expertise, and the opportunity to garner financial support to further develop key features of Native education activities.

L.A. Napier

To take action takes courage and strength. For when you take action you accept the
risk of being wrong and criticized—but not to try is the greater tragedy.

—L.A. Napier

One of the most significant problems we face as community members and
educators is how to improve the educational experiences of our children.
The model I designed for this chapter is about creating linkages that will allow us to break down existing barriers between communities. The question
mark in the center of my model represents the problem that needs to be addressed. The blocks in the upper right portion signify an institution of
higher learning. In the lower right area of the model are blocks that might
represent the public schools or Board of Indian Affairs (BIA) schools or
tribal schools. The blocks in the bottom left portion of the model signify the
community. It could be a tribal community, an urban community of Indian
people, or a reservation.

Each community (higher education, Indian community, and the school)
holds a piece of the puzzle. The puzzle is the problem, and we each hold a
piece of the solution for addressing the problem. Each community has an

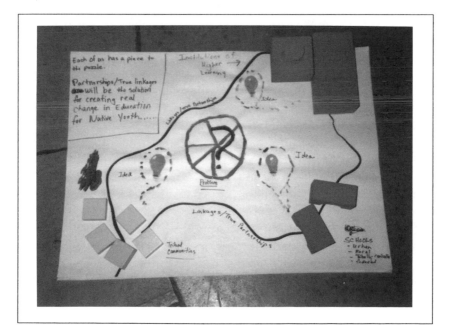

L.A. Napier's *Building Linkages Across the Community.*

idea. This is what the light bulbs portrayed in the model represent. Each light bulb represents an idea of how to solve one aspect of the problem.

One of the most significant barriers we face in education is that we are not communicating—we are not working together. At the University of Colorado in the school of education, we are attempting to create these linkages, or partnerships, between school districts and the communities we serve. In my own division of educational administration, we use action research, referred to as *problem-based learning*, as our link. The school becomes our client by contracting with us. Our university students work as research teams in addressing the problems the schools have identified. However, this is only one part of the partnership. We also hope to broaden this partnership by including the communities we serve. I don't feel we do enough of this yet, but we are getting there. At the higher education level, our students (who may be future principals) are working with the schools. We need to get them into the communities as well. It takes a great deal of effort to maintain these partnerships, for if one group is left out of the discussion the entire chain of communication can break down. This is why it is imperative to include all the communities that are served by both the school district and the institution of higher learning.

I think we know, generally, what constitutes the needs of our tribal communities. The 1970s and 1980s were filled with continuous studies and assessments identifying these needs. In the early 1990s, there was the White House conference on Indian Education, followed by the national report on the status of Indian education, *The Indian Nations At Risk* study. Our task now as educators, scholars, and community members is to share knowledge and practices that have been proven effective. We must also support one another in our individual and group attempts to take action. To take action takes courage and strength. For when you take action, you accept the risk of being wrong and criticized, but to not try is the greater tragedy.

One way you can begin to form these partnerships is to have an initial meeting with the local leaders from all the representative groups, to establish trust and rapport and discuss the purpose of the partnership. Establishing this initial rapport is very important. The next step might be to send out a request for proposals to the schools and communities asking what they think the biggest problem is that they would address first. It may be a safety or curricular issue, or a discipline policy that is no longer effective. For example, if it is a discipline issue, our school law action research team would meet with the community and school representatives to develop a new policy to meet both the needs of the community and state legislative mandates.

The concept of using action research to create and maintain linkages is fascinating and one I believe will work. The professors become resource gathers and not lecturers in ivory towers. We become facilitators between the groups involved. For example, we might say to our students, "These are the materials you should read in order to have the background necessary to address this problem. These are the individuals you should talk with first before addressing this issue." Many times the answers may not be in a book, but in the community, or with parents. Students have to make the effort to include all members of the community who are affected by this problem to find the answers. A problem education has had in the past is that people believed the schools had, or were, the answer. In turn, public schools blamed the parents, the parents blamed the teachers, the teachers blamed the administrators, and so on! A never-ending blame game. Communities involved in education believe if they had the right people representing them they could solve their problems. This just isn't true. We all have to work together, each member of the community has to take responsibility and be accountable to make education work for everyone in the next millennium.

A few examples of how our team, as representatives of the higher education community, created a link with tribal communities. I served on the Denver Public Schools American Indian Advisory Council. The board is made up of school representatives and community members. Because of our work together, we were able to submit a proposal to the Denver Public School Board to form several American Indian Focus Schools. Our collaborative effort was board-approved, and we are currently implementing the initiative.

The second example involves a tribe that was having teacher–student relationship problems in the public schools. A great deal of resentment was being voiced by all the parties involved. The students were having real learning problems in that school environment. Hence, the tribe wanted to create their own school, but they were not ready to proceed. Representatives of our institution were asked by both the school district and the tribe to act as liaisons between the two communities. We had several meetings with all parties concerned. We knew that the key to a successful partnership was trust among and between players. The tribal community needed to see us as an advocate and not a threat. I recall one tribal council member asking me, as a Native American woman researcher, what my motive was for being involved. She asked me if I was there to do research or write a grant? I understood her suspicion, and explained that my involvement was a way of paying back, to Native communities, the education I was fortunate to receive. I shared with her that if I had not received a fellowship from the Indian Education Act, I would never have earned a degree, never would have had the opportunity to be a university professor, and never have had the chance to support the work of Native people. I explained it was my way of giving back. I knew that trust between all of us was imperative if this highly volatile partnership would work. People have to know your motives—failing to explain why you want to help is the biggest mistake educators can make. The tribe is now in a position to form their own school but will continue to need support and assistance from other tribes and communities.

I can see how forming partnerships can work in small communities, as well as in large, urban areas. The message to take from this model is that we need to build linkages, and more importantly, maintain them. It takes everyone working together to make a difference.

'Umi kūmālua (Chapter 12)

Envisioning a Community-Centered Education: "We do not own our children, we must honor them in all ways."

Paul Johnson
Ojibwe Educator

Prologue

When Paul introduced his model, he began by asking the group to examine the political, structural, economic trends, and activities of their own unique communities. He pointed out that because the school is a part of the larger community it is influenced by as well as influences the directions and activities of the broader community. Understanding how one's school and school-related activities are situated within the social, economic, political, and physical community is essential toward gaining clarity and insight into school policies and practices.

For example, Paul observed, in some Native communities there exists attitudinal, economic, and structural barriers that limit Native student opportunities. Some communities, because their members have been so deeply affected by the boarding school experience or public school practices that have excluded Native history and culture, view schools today with distrust. Hence, gaining support for schools becomes a difficult task. Changing attitudes that are deeply embedded in a long history of colonialism requires intentional processes that seek to heal and provide hope. Economic barriers emerge around many different issues, but in particular, the effect of gaming on some Native groups has essentially shifted the community's focus to the development of economic infrastructures instead of schools. Finally, Paul wondered aloud if our Native schools are any different from non-Native schools. He suggested that because Native school leaders have not taken the time to integrate Native ways of knowing and behaving in their governing and decision making structures, many tribally controlled schools look and behave similarly to mainstream public school structures that have served to limit, and disenfranchise, Native children.

The message of Paul's vision is that at the heart of a holistic model for education is a healthy community. This became a guiding principle of the model Go to the Source. We are reminded that a healthy community is one where every individual is seen as an equal and all of its organizations are inclusive. A healthy community can build a healthy environment in which children and youth feel safe, can acquire a life-long passion for learning, and obtain the skills they need to succeed in their Native, and across non-Native, communities.

Paul Johnson (left) with Kalena Silva (right).

Paul Johnson's *Envisioning a Community-Centered Education.*

The model that I have constructed is one that I would like to see implemented in Michigan's Indian communities. It will take a great deal of reaffirming our own learning styles and changing our priorities to be successfully implemented. My proposed model puts the community at the center of educational policymaking. The circle design reinforces a traditional decision making concept of the Anishnabe people that encourages decision-making in a manner that insures that no one person or thing is viewed as superior to the other. All parts of the circle have equal importance. The circle represents the concept that all elements of the educational organization or decision making are inclusive rather than exclusive.

Until recently, tribal communities have always had their educational decisions prescribed for them. It is interesting that the state of Michigan prides itself in the belief that education is under the auspices of local control, and that our local communities can best determine the educational goals of their school district. Unfortunately, the state Board of Education and the legislature continue to place incentive requirements on our local school boards. These incentive requirements (whether implementing a core curriculum, accreditation standards, or special programs), are tied to monetary enticements. In the end, school districts are forced to meet the new requirements or face the loss of revenue. Local control is not happening in Michigan school districts.

The problem of local control is more complex for the Indian community. We are forced to deal with local school districts, the state Board of Education, state legislature, federal government, and in some cases, tribal governments. All have their beliefs about the education of Indian students. It's no wonder that although Anishnabe people want the best education for their children, we still have been unable to take full control of the education process in our communities. Our political strength is minimal when confronted with these powerful entities. For example, many local school boards in Michigan have few Native American members, so, our voice is often seen as an intrusion. Many of our Native students go to public schools, some go to Indian-controlled schools (tribal schools), and others to charter schools. As a result of our lack of influence, which results in little to no control over their education, Native students suffer. Fortunately, we are gaining some educational ground, albeit slowly.

Unfortunately, even on reservation communities where we have some control over the education of our students, we have difficulty defining and creating effective processes for achieving a quality education for our students. In our own Native communities, we have different beliefs concerning the education of our students. Very few Indian communities have taken the time to look at how we have, and how we should, develop our educational policies. As a result, we often create schools that put up barriers to success for our students.

With the advent of gambling in our communities, we have lost sight of the importance of education and are focusing on the infrastructure to support our economic development efforts. Although these activities are important, we cannot lose sight of the benefits of an educated Indian community. Many or our economic development activities have only created a new welfare system for our people. We must continue to set high educational expectations for our youth.

Currently, schools on the reservations have selected the charter school process, and as a result must adhere to the policies of the state. These policies have a dampening effect on our communities. We still do not have full control of curriculum, teacher and administrator certification, or student achievement issues. Full tribal control is not occurring. Tribal schools are often not recognized by the local school boards and very little collaborative work occurs. This results in competition for students and more often than not creates an adversarial situation between tribal and local schools.

The Indian community finds itself in the middle of these political structures and struggles. This fosters an environment where it is difficult to create change for the students. Indian community members must be at the center of educational decision-making. The community must generate thoughts and ideas such as "What it is that makes a strong, healthy Anishnabe child?" These important discussions must take place at the community level. Our people have had many educational experiences to draw on. Indian people know what is important and what their educational system should strive to do.

Many of our people have endured boarding school experiences, public and parochial school philosophies, the schools of hard knocks, and more recently, the college or university experience. Instead of using this knowledge, I fear too many of our communities surrender, and do not fight to determine the type of education their children should receive. To many of our concerned Indian educators and parents, it becomes very frustrating. Our lack of involvement demonstrates a feeling of nonconfidence in our abilities to decide what is best for our children.

My model is designed using a circle arrangement. I believe that everything that we do entails viewing the subject in a manner that makes sure that no one thing or person is seen as superior. The circle represents the concept that all organizations should be inclusive, rather than exclusive. In my model, I believe the center should be the community. It is the primary focus because this is where the thoughts and ideas about what it is that makes a strong, healthy, Ojibway child should be discussed, and where decisions should be made.

The next ring in the circle involves students. Often, the educational process will have students on the outer ring rather than where they should be, right next to the community. The Creator tells us that we do not own our children, that they have been given to us for only a short time, and that we must honor them in all ways. Because of their special status in our communities, we must include their ideas and thoughts. Many in our communities say they are meeting the needs of the students, but have not taken the time to include students in establishing educational policy. It is extremely important to include our students in the decision making process. I have seen successful parent groups and committees that include students from the age of 12.

The third ring of the model involves the school staff. Too often, our communities have allowed the school staff to make decisions about the education of their children with little to no input from others. We (parents and community members) must work with the education staff. We must teach them about our beliefs and values regarding education. Certainly, teacher training institutions have not trained the teachers and staff to teach Ojibway children. At the staff level, there are diverse skill levels. That is, some school personnel are still teaching from their "practice" teaching lesson plans, some have not taken the time to do any professional development, and then there are some who are just putting in their time. Whatever the situation, the school staff is extremely important. As community members, we must not forget our responsibilities as Indian parents, grandparents, aunt's and uncles to our students.

The fourth ring in my model represents programs. Programs should not run the educational system, but unfortunately the Native community will let the "wizards and gurus" come into our communities and say, "I have a program." They try to sell the community on particular programs, whether these be math, reading, or science programs, under the guise it will have our children performing at the highest academic levels. We spend a lot of money on these types of programs. Many become failed promises. We forget about creating our own programs.

Some of the best learning programs are created in-house and by individuals who are not formally schooled. Another concern I have about imported programs is that they are not culturally relevant. We cannot let the publishing companies come in and sell us a book and an idea. These books are based on someone else's assumptions and someone else's testing philosophy, which is usually not based on Ojibway values or experiences. My model puts a heavy burden on the community to maintain an educational focus and develop what it is that they want an Ojibway child to learn and exhibit.

The strands radiating from the middle are the curriculum issues that educational policies must address. They represent math, science, language, and reading. They can be anything that the school community decides or selects. Because the community decides, the model can have as many "spokes" radiating as they want. In my mind, we should have at least the four just mentioned (math, science, language, and reading). All of these spokes intersect in the model's center with the community. The community must realize that it has the ability to create and critique it's school's curriculum. The educational system must expend efforts to improve our students' spirit, body, and mind.

The thrust of the model is the community and the process of working outward rather than inward. Most of my model is about generating a curriculum that is culture-based, and is infused in everything. For example, most tribes use similar colors like red and black. The four colors that I used are red, yellow, blue, and green. The colors represent the four directions. To go beyond the Native studies concept is a separate subject. To me, in a lot of respects, it has held us back. Culturally based ideas should be integrated in all areas, rather than separating them. For example, the language and reading components should incorporate cultural values within the whole construct.

We must help communities understand that they have the ability to develop their own programs. It is the issue of resources that are within the community to develop education. Most of the time we only need to encourage them by saying, "Yeah, we can do it." For example, the ability to write curriculum is not a sacred science. You need to know what it is you want to teach, and from that point, develop activities that reinforce learning objectives. Then, one needs to devise methods to verify students have learned the concepts. Communities must develop their own culturally based curriculums.

Another component that is difficult for educators to include in their decision making is the student element. There are so many diversions, distractions, and factors that are prevalent on our reservations. We used to be isolated communities, but no longer. In our state, we have casinos, television, drugs, and gangs. We now have all of those things that educators have to deal with in the urban communities. Our youth workers need to reintroduce the clan system, of belonging to an extended family beyond your own nuclear family.

My vision is that Indian people will view the education of their students in a way where policies and ideas are generated at the community level. This vision is guided by the belief that recognizes that personal uniqueness and differences are to be valued and respected; that the sharing of one's perspective is not an aggressive act, but a gift to the community; that harmony and balance in the things that we do is not sameness; that each of us has a responsibility to our community, society, and the next seven generations; that all indigenous cultures have always been, and shall forever remain, important, valuable, and relevant; and that most of all, that we value our language, teachings, and ceremonies.

'Umi kūmākolu (Chapter 13)

The Circle We Call Community:
"As a community, you all have to pull together."

Miranda Wright
Doyon Foundation

Prologue

Miranda brought to our gathering a refined and eloquent mix of theoretical knowledge regarding leadership, practical experiences that taught important lessons about community development, and a passion for collecting and sharing the dynamic, traditional stories of Alaska's Native people. Although the indigenous peoples of the North Pacific region are unique and diverse, to include the Inupiat, Yup'ik, Tlingit, Haida, Tsimshian, Athabaskan, and Aluet societies, Miranda emphasized the need for all the different groups to define common needs around which a critical mass of expertise and funding could be granted. For example, the Doyon Foundation, which Miranda founded, in partnership with Native and non-Native groups, is determined to see that teachers learn more about the cultural and social environment of their indigenous students. This focus brought together Native and non-Native educators, school administrators and policymakers, community elders and leaders, and parents and families in active collaborations currently working to develop culturally appropriate learning activities. The importance of this foundation's work is twofold: First, the students' academic studies are now enriched with culturally appropriate activities which teach Native children about the environment and how to contribute to the physical and emotional strength of their community; and second, the family, the essential unit of a community, is integrally involved in the education of it's children and youth.

135

The lessons that stories tell, integrated into the traditional school curriculum, carry important messages in Miranda's model. Because the youth of the villages are literally the future life of the community, Miranda spoke passionately about how the traditional stories and ways of storytelling, can teach children and youth about the cultural richness of their heritage. Additionally, Miranda argued that Native stories are the paths that scholars must pursue to define an indigenous epistemology. The Yup'ik girl learns to tell stories that teach moral lessons and history with the Yup'ik story knife. This decorated stick or knife is used to draw pictures in wet dirt or snow that flow along with an oral story that is not scripted, but crafted to suit the audience. This is a skill, Miranda stated, that carries on the dynamic traditions of a rich culture, but also teaches us about the importance of orality, observation, and the connections between nature and man. Miranda's model is like a story knife, in that she has drawn a vision for us of education grounded in the creation story of the Athabaskan people.

What are common threads across diverse groups are not only the important issues of teacher education, curriculum development, and collection and teaching of stories, but also the ceremonies that meet universal needs of the human spirit. Through Miranda's model, the reader is reminded that access to all knowledge is imperative toward developing spiritual connections and understandings of how the past affects our present and future. The process of gaining knowledge, therefore, helps a child to think critically, to live in peace with the environment, and to seek health and well-being. The challenge, then, for Native educators, school administrators, community leaders and elders, parents and families, and students (children & youth), is to work together to build their community's capacity to protect their land, be life-long learners, and preserve their dynamic cultural richness.

Miranda Wright

As a community, you all have to pull together and when one member of that community leaves, there's a void.

—Miranda Wright

Miranda Wright's *The Circle We Call Community*.

The center of my model is the community. Here, I refer to *community* as an overarching structure that incorporates many interactions. One family could be a community. A village, or the town in which you live, is another form of community. Basic values such as education, cultural beliefs, learning, sharing are all part of a community. Everyone who lives in your community is a part of its infrastructure.

In this model, there are several pairs of a male and a female in various stages of cultural adaptations. Colors and feathers are used to differentiate the changes that occur. I begin with a set of elders, to establish a time sequence that demonstrates cultural change and social pressures on the community as a result of outside influences and contact with other cultures. The elders wear a feather headdress and have white arms. The white arms symbolize purity of thought and belief, an indicator that their culture and society is intact. The elders also represent the knowledge base of this community. They are the philosophers, doctors, and culture-bearers. Among my people, the *Athabaskan* of interior Alaska, we had traders who traveled across territorial boundaries. They brought back things like trade beads and other knowledge, but also, they shared our culture with others.

The next generation in the model is a male and female performer; people who sing, dance, and carry on the culture in whatever way their art determines. Notice the subtle changes on the performers compared to the elders. The headdress is smaller and the arms of the performers are brown. This indicates an infusion, or adaptation, as a result of outside influences, but manifestations of the culture are still present.

The third pair, or generation, is not wearing a headdress. There are cars, and other influences of the dominant culture, present. This generation is fraught with confusion and is searching for an identity. The fourth generation incorporates bright colors and glitter with the emergence of traditional manifestations, such as the small headdress. This generation represents an acknowledgment of their heritage combined with an acceptance and adaptation of outside influences. Although the people can adapt to fast cars, and the many influences of another society, they attempt to maintain their unique ethnicity.

The rounded blocks in the model represent traditional dwellings. The flow of activity in these dwellings is circular, thus, the rounded blocks. Likewise, activity in these dwellings centered on the fire pit, or hearth. Symbolically, the domed roof of these structures can be equated to the overarching community discussed earlier in the presentation of this model. As outside pressures come to bear, the dwellings also change. People are moving into framed buildings, that I refer to as "cracker boxes." Much effort is spent on adapting to the dominant culture. However, survival as a people is near impossible. Many Native people feel a need to retain their culture as a means of identity. Although many people live in a large modern community, they have found ways to structure their traditional community within the overarching model.

When I first worked with the concept of community involvement in education, I focused on several elders who were employed as "cultural resources" in their local schools. Discussions with these elders revealed that several were unsure of their contribution to classroom teaching. As one elder stated, "I don't know what they want me down there [at school] for. I don't know how to share my information with them. She had a difficult time trying to plan a meaningful presentation for the students and give them something of value. We started talking about the seasons in our lives and the different things we can do with seasons. It was like the light bulbs came on for her! She said, "Oh, now I understand. That's what I will do. I will take that circle and I'll put the seasons into it. For example, when we talk about activities on the Yukon River in June, we talk about them differently in our language. The words that we use for the Yukon River and the activities associated with that river are different. To present her lessons, she incorporated Native language and cultural activities associated with the different seasons of the year.

I went back to the University of Alaska and worked with other Native educators there. We started exploring different models and looking at the cyclical nature of activities and how they progressed from one stage to another throughout the year. We divided the circle into four quadrants representing spring, summer, fall, and winter. The basic premise was to use the four seasons as a vehicle for discussion. The seasons allow for cyclical change: birth, growth, maturity, and reflection, much like the birth of new plants and animals in spring, the growth associated with summer, the maturity, or harvest, of fall, and the reflection and celebrations during winter.

The first quadrant was called spring, the time of renewal. In order to capture the essence of our efforts, we decided to refer to our creation legends for an appropriate Native word that would add depth to our model. We discussed several creation legends and found a common thread ... the presence of a primordial being or spiritual essence. This provided further discussion on the sequence of creation according to traditional legends. Thus, the first quadrant was called *yeegah* to reflect the spiritual essence, or, visionary phase, found in our creation narratives. This first phase provides a time to explore your thoughts, to develop a vision for the future, and to establish your introduction, or outline. Moving sun-wise around the circle to the second quadrant, we experience growth during the summer season. Again relying on traditional stories, we learned that land was created before man or animals. Thus, we named the second quadrant *nen* to reflect the formation of the earth. This is a period of growth, a time to develop different programs, different skill levels, and so forth.

Again moving sun-wise around the circle, we come to the third quadrant, or, the period of maturity and harvest. Again referring to the creation legends, we associated this period with the emergence of man or humankind, *Denaa*. As my grandmother would say;

> Koy [grandchild] right here is *Denaa*, this is man. Over here are the animals. We used to be one, and we would travel back and forth through each other's worlds. Something happened and we split. This is the real people, this is *Denaa*.

According to our distant time stories, it is during this separation with the animal kingdom that *Denaa* developed knowledge, critical thinking, and language. Consequently, the fall cycle is referred to as *"Denaa."* This is the phase where instruction and development of the knowledge base is implemented. The final quadrant, or winter season, is a period of reflection and evaluation. A time to measure the activities of the year and prepare to renew the cycle. This phase is associated with content and accomplishment, and is, therefore, referred to as *Tlee*. The literal translation is *head*. However, it is also used to specify the head as the fountain of knowledge.

This seasonal model based on our creation stories has worked very well for us. A nice feature of the circular model is the progressive element, or automatic reconnection, associated with the annual renewal or cyclical changes. This model can be superimposed on or in another circle indefinitely to create the different communities within an overarching structure. I've found it to be a wonderful tool to demonstrate the infrastructure within an organization, classroom, family, or community where everyone and everything reconnects. Another analogy that I have used is the blanket toss, that is similar to jumping on a trampoline. However, with the blanket toss there are no springs to elevate the individual jumping. Instead, people form a circle around the blanket and pull it tight. Everyone has to pull in unison in order to get the jumper to rise as high as they can. If anyone is out of sync, the jumper cannot be elevated any higher. Likewise, as a community we all have to pull together, and when one member of the community leaves, there is a void.

I have always enjoyed the storytelling ability of my people and their ability to apply the events of a story as a lesson for various challenges that people face. The same story may be repeated several times, depending on the current situation. The reason behind the repetition was obviously lost on those who continue to perceive indigenous storytelling as lacking in academic value. Many equate the indigenous style of storytelling with a mentality of children, who must learn by rote memorization. Consequently, these Native stories are often relegated to the folklore section of the library, never to be validated as a valuable source of knowledge.

There are many cultural preservation efforts directed at gathering and recording our elders. The idea behind many of these efforts is that traditional information will be lost with the passing of the elder. Therefore, it is imperative that we preserve the stories of their life, histories, songs, stories and so forth. I find it interesting that industry has reaped tremendous financial profits from sales of recorders, audiotapes, and videotapes, so the amateur can build an archive of information that generates another financial investment as we collect (and attempt to understand) the complexities of preserving information. In discussing this phenomenon, I pose the questions, "What is it that we are preserving?" And, "How long must it be kept in preservation?" I an image of our cultural heritage locked in a jar with a shelf life stamped on a label, "Use before Nov. 11, 2001."

Some may feel that I am being profane in discussing the knowledge of our elders in this fashion. I, on the other hand, want to stress the importance of sharing and using the information to perpetuate a living, dynamic culture. What good is the collection of knowledge if it is stored merely for posterity? Our youth are at risk as many struggle with a lack of identity or a sense of false pride. One often hears the phrase, "I'm proud to be Indian." When probed further about what it is that makes them proud of their heritage, many are at a loss to express or articulate what it is that makes them proud, whereas others take the noble warrior attitude, and become defensive. Yet, their response is indicative of their need for an identity. This example can be taken a level further, to those encouraging us to learn from our elders. However, when probed about what it is they want to learn from the elders, they are at a loss to identify or articulate what knowledge they seek. These examples suggest that knowledge of their heritage is so lacking they do not know what questions to ask. Perhaps the western educational system has had such a dramatic impact on our Native population that our youth do not know how to frame their inquiries from an indigenous perspective. An example that illustrates this is the occurrence at a potlatch hosted by a community–village to honor the elders, who congregated for their annual conference:

> During the period when speeches are made, the Native leaders of this community welcomed the elders and spoke of the honor they felt in hosting such a distinguished group, particularly in light of the fact that most of their Native elders had passed on to their next journey. By hosting this event they hoped to gain knowledge from the elder present. With that said, an elder from a nearby community rose, and asked in traditional Athabaskan oratory style, "Where are your young men? Where are your hunters?" He posed these questions as he observed young girls (ages 8–13) serving the elders, a position traditionally reserved for the hunters, who provided the game meat and fish for such ceremonies. The speaker went on to explain the purpose of his questions. The same community spokesperson, who previously asked for the elders' assistance and access to cultural knowledge, rose and disputed the elder who offered assistance.

This lack of understanding for the protocol at traditional ceremonies led to my probing further where the balance of understanding could be met. I fear the Western education system has provided at least two generations of students with the tools to evaluate their surroundings through the eyes of Western traditions. If this is true, our task as Native educational leaders is extremely challenging. Where and how do we provide a mechanism to present a balanced education for our youth to meet the needs of the 21st Century, but still be linked to their traditional culture? These are the types of concerns that lead me to focus my direction on the teaching and learning styles of indigenous communities. The task that lies before us is great.

In response to this challenge, I'm currently working with several certified Native teachers and we have formed the Association of Interior Native Educators (AINE). This focus group, in collaboration with the Doyon Foundation, where I serve as executive director, is the cornerstone of an initiative, The Academy of Elders, intensive, 2-week, summer institutes where certified teachers become the students and elders serve as the instructors. The Academy of Elders summer institute is in its fourth year. Elders from various communities work with teachers to develop curriculum that implements the teaching and learning styles of the indigenous people. The curriculum incorporates stories, hands-on activities, and songs with performance and academic standards established by the state department of education. Additionally, teacher-training components are being developed in conjunction with the University of Alaska to ensure the success of this program. Rather than looking at the differences we have as Native people, we take a global look at the educational needs of our children and youth. Just as each student is an individual, so, too, do they learn independently. Rather than immediately diagnosing Native American students who experience learning challenges as having attention deficit disorder (ADD), more work is needed for educators to understand the cooperative teaching and learning methods common to many indigenous cultures. Educators need to understand the importance of building their lessons on the cultural and social environment of their students and in the community in which they work.

This initiative brings together Native and non-Native educators, school administrators and policymakers, community elders and leaders, and parents and families, in active working collaborations. The importance of this work is multifaceted: first, students become the focus of the classroom as teachers incorporate various teaching methods that address the variety of learning styles in the classroom. Second, students are enriched with culturally appropriate activities that teach them about their environment. Third, the family, an essential unit of a community, is integrally involved as a cultural resource to the consortia and to the ultimate education of their children and youth. Finally, the unified effort of this model contributes to the physical and emotional strength of all the communities involved.

'Umi kūmāha (Chapter 14)

Educational Empowerment for Maori People: "We are on the right path. We are on the right dreaming."

Susan Wetere-Bryant
Director, LIFEworks New Zealand

Prologue

As a child, Maenette's kupuna told her that the making of a flower lei for someone special was a blessed gift. Her knowing and working with Susan felt much like receiving a very lovingly created flower lei. Both Joanne and Maenette can still feel the warm caresses of her embrace, the sweet scent of her passionate belief in her people, and the simplicity and wisdom in her words. As an educational leader, Susan worked diligently to create learning environments for disenfranchised Maori and non-Maori youth and young adults. With a master's degree in education that is based on adult learning and teaching, she has been able to employ her research, evaluation, and organizational skills in championing several major community and urbanwide projects that focus on health, vocational, and employment education. Currently, she is building a youth and young adult leadership initiative that partners with Native leadership programs across the globe.

The overriding message of Susan's model is that Native education should be grounded in self-pride and empowerment. Like Jeannette Armstrong, Susan believes that every youth must be given an opportunity to succeed, learn, grow, and contribute to their community. In fact, Susan states that if one is Maori, and born in New Zealand, one is mandated to work hard! Susan's model interweaves the elements of critical intellectual development, physical well being, cultural and language knowledge, and spiritual connections around social transformation. That is, her story begins with the challenge that all educational models must encourage ways of doing that assures the restoration, development, and survival of cultural knowledge and language. She also pointed out that, partnered with cultural knowledge, students must also have global knowledge so they can create social change in contemporary society. All this is wrapped up in solid leadership, which she believes is a process that manifests real movement for Maori people.

Susan with daughters Hanna, Elle, and husband, Ady

Maori education is about awakening understandings and meanings about the unique worldview we have as Maori. It is about creating meanings that serve our people, now and in the future, continue our language, culture and traditions, provide skills for a local and global economy, and nurture whilst also empowering. Right now the Maori people are coming together to rejuvenate. I think if you're a Maori, born in New Zealand, you're very lucky.

You're born with a mandate to work hard for your people. It's an understanding we have that we're here for each other, because we have all rights
to our country. In another 20 years, probably 50% of New Zealand's population will have Maori blood. We're growing ourselves! And, we see exciting
opportunities.

For successful education practices, there are several principles I believe
need to be met. First, all learning needs to involve the concepts of the past,
present, and future. All learning needs to be delivered with a balance of the
physical, mental and spiritual levels of understanding. We also need to center our learning around understanding oneself, one's environment, and the
relationship between oneself and one's environment, as a means to access
knowledge. Central to all teaching must be the belief that all knowledge is
accessible, it is the questions that are asked, and the frames of intellectual
reference that are developed, that determine how knowledge is integrated
within an individual.

As teachers and leaders, we have the responsibility of supporting others
to develop those frames of reference. We need to empower our people
through discussing how meanings are created and how culture and language are part of that meaning creation. If a school, primary or secondary, is
based on principles pertaining to culture and language, as well as community involvement, it will live and breathe the concepts of love, of sharing,
and of giving. The core principles of learning should include laughter, humor, and an understanding of everything related to Native philosophy.

The destruction of our language, culture, and ways of being Maori
through colonization has disenfranchised several generations of our people.
But it has also provided an opportunity to rebuild meaning as a people. A
meaning that is growing incredibly, a worldview, which is a oneness of living, a connectedness between people. This is a good time to talk about the
women in my model. In the model, there are six women from both past and
present who represent principles of thinking and action, that I believe
should underpin our educational systems. Beginning from the past to the
present, I reflect on what each woman brings to our learning and our work
today.

The heart of my model is the birth of life. When you *hongi* someone (the
pressing of the noses) you're sharing the essence of life. When you say
Kiaora it means to live, to be well, to be healthy, and to love. At the top of
the model is *Te Puea*, she was one of this centuries' greatest Maori leaders.
She led her people through major turbulent times after World War II, economic depression, *pakeha* (White) settlement, and land alienation. She was

Susan Wetere-Bryant's *Educational Empowerment for Maori People.*

a great believer in the idea that a community was only as good as its poorest member, therefore, everyone had a responsibility to uplift the socioeconomic status of others in their community. Te Puea had great visions of what Maori people could achieve, and believed in holistic, economic, educational, political, and social development.

Herapo Rongo, the middle left photo, and Maggie Papakura, the middle right photo, followed Te Puea. Herapo, as a young woman, had seen her people's land taken from them to create *pakeha* settlements. She vowed to see the day that it would be returned. She devoted her life to this cause and succeeded. In her late 70s, she witnessed the return of many homelands. Herapo held firmly to her cultural knowledge and heritage, and worked devotedly serving justice for her people.

Maggie Papakura was New Zealand's first postgraduate fellow at Oxford University; one of the first Maori to chart new ground in England's closed academic halls. Maggie completed her thesis on Native flora and fauna, concentrating on the healing properties known to Maori. Her work provides an example of how foreign educational systems can be used to enhance Maori knowledge. She also demonstrated how Maori people could work in a foreign environment and hold strong to their culture and language.

A generation later, we come to our current leaders: Denise Henare, Paparangi Reid, and June Jackson. Denise is a lawyer specializing in Maori land and development. Paparangi is a medical doctor working as a research leader in Maori public health. And, June Jackson is an urban pan–tribal authority leader. All women have carved their destinies to serve Maori advancement. Through their work, they have transformed attitudes toward Maori issues and engineered change in communities, firmly grounding Maori knowledge in their work. It is difficult to do justice to these women in the few words I share here. Their achievements, their principled actions rooted in Maori values and beliefs, their work for social justice that utilizes all avenues of knowledge to enlighten, are examples of the essence of what our Maori educational system must mean and contribute. From the work of all these women we learn that we must believe our success is only as good as the success of others.

My family, of the tribe Ngati Maniapoto, established a *Wananga*, which is similar to the Tribal colleges in the United States. The Wananga was founded by my father, Rongo Wetere, in response to increasing unemployment of young Maori. He went across all tribal boundaries to set it up, with a singleminded determination. We actively target, and attract, Maori who have been labeled by the system as educational failures. Maori who are mostly low-skilled, in lower socioeconomic levels, and who have seemingly lost their roots. We do not see these labels, we see only people who are bursting with talent, energy, and who are able to thrive in a nurturing, culturally attuned environment. The achievements in learning are incredible. The Wananga strives to rise above all societal, economic, and educational barriers, and are quite successful. The school provides vocational skills qualifications and Maori culture education. We have dance, singing, carving, painting, language, and culture classes. There is also development of communication and social skills.

There are three Wananga in Aotearoa, each built by the commitment of three men, their *whanau* (family) and tribes. It has taken years of lobbying and political changes to achieve what has been done. We will no doubt need to continue to do so. Wananga is not accepted well in today's tertiary environment. Universities tend not to acknowledge us. We are seen as organizations who deal with "that sector," the ones that the mainstream can't cope with. What has been their weakness, though, is our strength.

Another example of our work is an institution that was built on a rubbish site [laughter]! Today, it turns over millions of dollars, and trains thousands of our people. It takes people who have graduated from secondary school and helps us to refine our Maori language skills and knowledge of our culture. We can learn about a number of other topics, but of greatest values is learning how to work with our own people, on the grassroots level, to create social change. It's given people like me and others an opportunity to build important programs. Like I said earlier, the universities in New Zealand don't acknowledge the Wananga. Because we work with students who are considered by others to be "hard nuts to crack," we have to provide the learning experience in a more appropriate way. Therefore, we don't teach as the university might. We integrate Maori ceremony, language, values, and teaching to all our skill training.

In regard to today's education, much emphasis is placed on structural-thinking models, ideas, concepts, variables, and definitions. In my work, I have realized that our people see things in terms of oneness. They have difficulty seeing the depth, color, variation, and factors. They see and breathe a landscape of knowledge in its entirety. My people struggled with me to accept the knowledge I had to share. I soon learned that I had to draw on the strength of seeing meaning in oneness and prepare my information and knowledge in a way that it could better be integrated into a particular context. I now believe we can learn anything we want if it is shared and directed in a way that the learner can integrate it into their own context.

There are many struggles in the development of better learning and teaching for our indigenous children. There are many philosophies and ways of thinking that need to be thought through. Every struggle and challenge adds to our development. Central to our success is valuing ourselves through knowing ourselves. We cannot fail if we are supported to access our inner strength, inner *mana* (self-power) we have to be effective in our lives.

Leadership in these efforts are key. To be an educational leader is a completely absorbing responsibility. I believe that I am an instrument through which energy is channeled. In this way, I am able to engage others to support their work or to help them understand their internal and external worlds. I see myself as an educational leader in the Maori community and at the government level. My role is to understand the Maori worldview as well as the non-Maori view. Then, as the cultural negotiator, make sense of it for both sides. I traverse worlds with an insider and outsider knowing, but with a goal to advance positive thinking and action that invests in Maori people.

I believe it is most important that we tap into our Native, and even a more universal, indigenous knowledge base, and begin to acknowledge that this is a divine gift. We need to also choose carefully where we place our energies. We need to ask ourselves where we can put our energies that they will have the most impact for the most people today and over time. We need to seek insight, and invest our energies where we feel it is right. Rightness is very important, but to feel it we must let go of fear and rationality, and let our energy force guide us. The answers are held in every breath we take.

'Umi kūmālima (Chapter 15)

Locating Global Learning Centers: *"With the united forces of us all."*

Rosalie Medcraft
Department of Education and the Arts,
Tasmania, Australia

Prologue

Rosalie, an Aboriginal Tasmanian, was one of the grandmothers in our gathering who shared unique information about her Tasmanian community roots. We learned that Dutch navigator Abel Tasman's arrival in 1642 brought an end to the Aboriginal Tasmanian's 12,000 years of isolation, the beginning of land wars, and the loss of unique languages and Aboriginal identity. Prior to European contact, the Tasmanian Aboriginal lived in small hearth groups consisting of approximately 11 related family members (on average). These hearth groups would join and make up a band of about 50 people, and led by a warrior-hunter. Like the Australian Aboriginals and indigenous people of New Zealand, Hawai'i, and North America, the people of Tasmania are deeply connected to their land. However, conflicting understanding about the meaning of land caused rifts between the Aboriginal people and the new settlers. The arrival of European settlers in 1803, brought the first massacre, in 1804, of Aboriginal Tasmanians at Risdon Cove. The struggle for land continued with the poisoning of Aboriginal people, abduction of children, and the rape of women. By 1830, the "Black Line." a military operation that formed a human chain across the European settled land of Tasmania, removed the last remaining Aboriginal Tasmanians. Most displaced Aboriginal people were transferred to either Oyster Cove Reserve or the Bass Strait Islands. By the 1850s, the Aboriginal community in the Bass Strait Islands sought recognition and land rights from the Tasmanian Government. By 1912,the Tasmanian Government established the Cape Barren Island Reserve Act, that returned blocks of land to the indigenous people.

Although the history of Aboriginal Tasmanians is rife with oppression, Rosalie explained that recent changes in Tasmanian governance have rekindled the hopes of a better future. For example, the influence of European contemporary culture brought new technologies and new ways of thinking to formal education, that, at its start, was for the most part devoid of Aboriginal history and language. During the 1970s, however, Aboriginal groups began to form political organizations that fought for Aboriginal rights to land, better housing and living conditions, and more control over decisions that directly affected their communities. By the 1990s, the government established the Aboriginal and Torres Strait Islander Commission (ATSIC) to administer Aboriginal programs. Today, Rosalie explained, Aboriginal people are seeking more culturally and language-appropriate education for their children. Rosalie also shared a quote, from a White author, that has impacted the Tasmanian Aborigine's work toward self-determination:

> Until we give back to the Black man just a bit of the land that was his and give it back without provisos, without strings to snatch it back , without anything but compete generosity of spirit in concession for the evil we have done to him—until we do that, we shall remain what we have always been so far: A people without integrity, not a nation, but a community of thieves. (Xavier Herbet, 1978)

Rosalie's model illuminates her people's struggle for self-determination and identity. She reminds us that love for our children is an essential foundation in whatever work we do. Like all the educational leaders who have shared their stories in this book, Rosalie too, talks about the fragility of Native education and how careful Native leaders must be as they address both internal and external barriers. Although Rosalie dreams of a global center where indigenous people can learn from one another, she is fully cognizant that what we must first learn to do is listen to one another. "Sometimes," she said an interview, "we're too busy yelling that we can't hear the birds, the ocean, and the land." Rosalie reminds us, through her transcripts and letters, how awesome the world really is, and what tremendous work Native leaders could do if they listened.

Rosalie Medcraft

It is today's students who will take up the challenge of ensuring a society that values Aboriginal people and cultures alongside all Australian people and cultures.

—Rosalie Medcraft

ROSALIE'S MODEL FOR EDUCATION

I am a guide. The Aboriginal educational system, in Australia, is an enormous challenge. I have been thinking about what we do in our educational system and comparing it to what I've heard others, in the United States and New Zealand, do. We are fortunate that we have Aboriginal studies in our curriculum, but the teaching is inconsistent. There are some teachers who are gung-ho, while others think, "I'm not going to touch it!" There's a majority who are saying, "How can we do this?" Because there are many teachers in opposition to Aboriginal studies, as curriculum specialists we are called to give them guidance. Reaching out to teachers is both a challenge

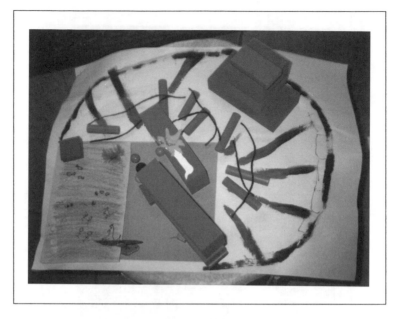

Rosalie Medcraft's, *Locating Global Learning Centers*

and a joy. Yet, the pride of the people in my community and their willing-ness and eagerness to learn about our history, language, and heritage is a great joy to me. At last, we are going forward instead of backward. The en-couragement of my family and work colleagues also gives me joy. We all can continue to grow and rise above adversity.

My vision is global. My thoughts are that indigenous education should be taught around the world, hence, the circle depicting the globe. I looked all around for a simple spot to place my model and found this drum. To be honest, when I started, I did not have the foggiest notion of what I would do, but here we are, learning from one another. This is what it should be like, all of us from around the world learning from one an-other. From all areas, our paths lead to this area of learning. We may not come from around the world, but we could come together from areas of each country or city. Just inside the circle, are blue and red blocks depict-ing educational institutions as they are today; just buildings. The blocks are in a pile that begins with one very small block, and the blocks grow in size, getting bigger and bigger. This represents indigenous learning, and indigenous education. It began very small, but hopefully, it will eventu-ally grow very big around the world.

The paths lead to an archway, the new learning areas. These paths start off black, but get brighter in color as the indigenous people come into the central learning area where people from all races unite as one. The indigenous people are depicted by the different colored beads. The blocks on the left (red) represent the education building, green and brown spaces represent the main learning areas, because I'm a great believer that our history and culture needs to be taught outside whenever practical. I have used small blue blocks to depict the lakes or oceans, and a gorgeous, happy sun is sitting on top of the archway. The sun is smiling down on indigenous learning, Aboriginal education, and all the people involved. Without the sun, the giver of life, we would have nothing. It's shining down on all of us here on Mother Earth. This is the main thrust of my model.

Something else; the lines that cross those paths and those around long blocks, are barriers that have been in the way of indigenous people and their learning, barriers that have been put up. Notice that some of them have been knocked down so that educators and students can pass through the archway. In Australia, racism is rampant, but it is nowhere near as bad as it has been. It is getting better. Another barrier is the educational system. Today, indigenous education is more acceptable. That is how we came to write the Aboriginal Studies guidelines and the government has made it compulsory for schools to teach Aboriginal studies. Education is turning around. Some teachers are afraid to teach the Aboriginal studies curriculum because they are frightened that if they say something wrong, they might upset an Aboriginal activist. Teachers, on the whole, are becoming more aware of unacceptable terms and stereotypes that have been prevalent.

There are barriers that indigenous people create. We have plenty of activists around. It's all about jumping up and down and getting on some bandwagon, "You should do this!" and "We shouldn't do that!" We may need "shaking up," but it can make my work difficult. Although I'm knocking down barriers in the school system, there are Aboriginal people building those walls again. It's quite sad. Aboriginal people need to support one another. When I was growing up, my father would not acknowledge his own Aboriginal lineage. We weren't allowed to talk about it. When we asked why our grandma was different, we were told that her family came from New Zealand. Many years later we discovered that was not so, but my Dad stuck to his story. It took almost 7 years of research to discover our true identity. When we were kids, we lived in a very small country town. If a stranger got off the train and came walking down the road, my dad would say, "You kids, get inside!" We thought we had a mean father, but perhaps he acted that way because Aboriginal children were being stolen from their families and given to other people—mostly to be treated no better than little slaves. It was terrible, but it was happening everywhere.

I've been thinking about that experience for some time. There are barriers like self-denial, which is what my father felt, that we must overcome. And there are barriers from the outside, too! I was getting quite upset one morning feeling that there are too many barriers—barriers everywhere, visual barriers, unseen barriers, and internal barriers—there are barriers in my vision for education. It is like a fence, and indigenous education is a fragile object trying to rip through. The indigenous people need to learn as much as possible. We need to learn from the land, we need to listen to each other. Sometimes I feel that I'm not listening. I think Aboriginal education should teach how to listen.

The barriers, built by non-indigenous people, are not insurmountable. How do we knock them down? Parents should be encouraged. Whenever possible, the educators should be the community elders and teachers the "special lessons." The majority of the teaching and learning should be done outdoors whenever possible. Parents could be involved by forming a group of "mother's helpers" to work with the teacher. All this involvement is important.

I have 6 children, 14 grandchildren, and 1 great-granddaughter who is 18 months old. Among my grandchildren, I have 8 grandsons and 6 granddaughters from age 24 to age 5. Back home, I went for a walk along the beach collecting shells and driftwood. My daughter-in-law is to visit a school to work where the children do craft work with the shells. As a family, we go camping at Christmas time. I reserve a place near the ocean, because to me, the sea is just magnificent. I live near the sea, too! I am attracted to it. My children's love is always with me. As Aboriginal leaders, we must keep our children close to us.

Afterword

Beatrice Medicine
Research Anthropologist Emeritus,
California State University, Northridge

As a retired academic, I am somewhat perturbed by the joint authorship of a volume that purports to present indigenous views of the educational enterprise. It is somewhat problematic to discern what is Aboriginal or non-Aboriginal in the introduction and transition sections. Fortunately, the bulk of the volume is written by indigenous people. The strength of this book lies in that fact. The Native authors wrote from their own personal experiences and this reflexivity is mirrored in the models they present.

This extraordinary collection of indigenous educators from Australia, New Zealand, Tasmania, the United States, and Canada are innovative leaders in their respective fields. However, the postcolonial question remains—How will self-determining Aboriginal educators meet their own needs and the aspirations of their constituencies via various educational structures? They courageously attempt to focus on this perennial paradox. It seems an enigma through centuries of colonial domination, education has been used by imperialist nations as a means of the assimilation of Native peoples to European cultures. A dominant society's culture, value system, and mercantile orientation has been held as the ideal way of life. Various methods of cultural domination is pervasive in all previously mentioned countries, with varying degrees of racism, classism, and Christianity to supplant Native belief systems. Suppression of indigenous cultures, languages, and Native rituals were part of the forced culture change that all endured—either individually, or, as a part of a Native heritage.

New social institutions with differing world views, value systems, kinship structures, and elements of expressive cultures—art, music, histories—were superimposed. Yet, Native cultures have persisted in varying forms and manifestations. Adaptive strategies were constructed to meet the needs of the indigenous nations. It is from these perjuring aboriginal groups that the contributors have emerged and have articulated their means of ingenious adaptations. The authors of the educational models present a rich experimental range of purposive action to make education more meaningful and satisfying. Many have "gone through the system," and have emerged with a variety of concepts that have been, in some cases, actualized. Educational experiences for students, they posit, can make a difference if they are based on indigenous worldviews and methods of teaching and learning. The underlying assumption is to "go to the source"—the community. Contours of the community ranges from a family to global village with a range of typologies in between.

Most of the models are symbolic and make interesting visual images. They reflect the author's experiences and the cultural heritage from which each contributor emanates. The models are extremely varied (as one might expect from such a disparate group). Some are emotive accounts of the participant's experience in cultural learning or relearning. Others are accounts of mediators, teachers, administrators, and professors. All seem to suggest that Native language knowledge is essential for effective teaching and learning. It would be helpful to know how many of these persons know the Native language of their group. Language and cultural revitalization seems at the core of many of these models. The degree of representativeness of Native cultural heritage is clear in some accounts and peripheral in others.

One must read and assess each contribution to determine this orientation and to weigh the usefulness of the model. Some models are evidences of actual working, effective modes of teaching. Some are tentative statements of idealistic visions. If these models are envisioned as devices in influencing new approaches in educational epistemology and methodology, a concretization in an institutional frame with possible replication or adaptation needs to be further analyzed, actualized, and evaluated. Otherwise, we are overwhelmed with individual idiosyncratic verbalizations with spirituality and community as vague and ephemeral categories. Certainly, spirituality is a private and protected value for most aboriginal peoples throughout the world. In these days of protection of traditional knowledge, intellectual property rights, and cultural appropriation, one must be careful as to how indigenous models are constructed and offered in the educational enterprises. The question remains in this postmodern age—How can these models be useful in communities of aboriginal peoples and in educational institutions of a dominant culture in which all indigenous peoples of the world interact?

The answer lies in this unusual, valuable volume. A wide range of committed, Native educators who, through experience, determination, and training, have enlarged their concern for their constituencies and have shared their models with other educators. It is for the latter to hone and select the most efficacious to their needs.

Appendix A

Exemplary Native Educational Programs in the United States

Browning High School
P. O. Box 610
Browning, MT 59417
(406) 338-2745
Fax: (406) 338-2844
Elaine Wilmot, Student Affairs Advisor

Browning High School enhances the preservation of Blackfeet culture, language, and traditions by requiring their students to take one semester of Native American studies with an emphasis on the Blackfeet Nation. The course encourages students to value and continue Blackfeet oral traditions, music, games, contests, arts and crafts, drumming, singing, and history of the tribe. Determined to promote the continuation of the Blackfeet culture and respect for all Native American tribes, Browning requires all teachers to take three graduate-level credits in Native American studies before they are given a third teaching contract.

Bug-O-Nay-Ge-Shig School
Route 3, Box 100
Cass Lake, MN 56633
(218) 665-2282
Fax: (218) 665-2286
Patty Cornelius, Superintendent
Carol Bliss, Gifted and Talented Program Coordinator

Founded in 1976, the Bug-O-Nay-Ge-Shig school, a Blue Ribbon school, is located on the Leech Lake Indian Reservation in Minnesota. The Bug-O-Nay-Ge-Shig School is a K–12 school serving 535 Ojibwe students. It is nationally recognized for implementing the elementary gifted and talented program, an exemplary academic program that consists of activities that assist students in achieving their full potential in the areas of leadership, critical thinking, academics, technology, and visual arts. The school is regarded as a model for its culturally appropriate curriculum design and assessment.

Chief Leschi Schools
School to Career Partnership Program
5625 52nd Street
East Puyallup, WA 98374
(206) 840-3892
Norm Dorpat, Director of Development

Chief Leschi school, located in Tacoma, Washington, serves 800 students in grades pre-K through 12. The School to Career Partnership Program was established to give all students' experiences pertinent to early career choices by having a strong connection between school and work-based learning. The program's objectives include making connections with community resources and agencies; presenting meaningful opportunities that enhance life skills; and creating a cultural environment that stimulates youth to value and achieve the characteristics of a productive and independent citizen. A method of connecting with the community includes learning programs and services that are sensitive to the culture of the students and community.

Choctaw After-School Program
P. O. Box 6010
Philadelphia, MS 39350
(601) 656-5251
Fax: (601) 656-7077
Mattie Mae Brown, Director

Choctaw Central High School, established in 1963, was a Bureau of Indian Affairs operated school until it became a Bureau of Indian Affairs Contract school on July 1, 1990. The After-School Program serves students ages 5 through 14. Included in the program are numerous activities that address culture, academics, physical fitness and psychomotor skills, and literacy through individual journals. The educational and social benefits realized by the Choctaw After-School Program include a decrease in drug and alcohol use, daily tutoring services that have increased academic achievement, a boost in school attendance, and the promotion and appreciation of Native culture.

Choctaw Tribal Schools
Choctaw Technology Education Program (CTEP)
P. O. Box 6008
Philadelphia, MS 39350
(601) 656-0793
Rick Smith, Instructional Technologies Coordinator

The Choctaw Tribal Schools are located 69 miles north of Jackson, Mississippi on the Choctaw reservation. The Choctaw Technology Education Program provides computer-based, electronic network resources to assist in the professional development of teachers within the Choctaw Tribal Schools System. The performance objectives are twofold; the first, that teachers will increase their use of instructional technologies across various disciplines in K–12 classrooms, and second, to promote meaningful, relevant, computer-based instruction to Choctaw Indian students.

Cibecue Community School
Main Street
P. O. Box 80068
Cibecue, AZ 85911
(520) 332-2444
Fax: (520) 332-2341
Ron Shaw, Principal
Michelle Thomas, Curriculum Coordinator

The Cibecue Community School is a K–12 educational grant school committed to integrating Native culture into the school curriculum. Located on the White Mountain Apache reservation, the school offers projects and programs to promote bilingualism and biculturalism. Some of their exemplary projects include an intensive Grave's writing workshop for grades 1–8 to increase literacy and English proficiency, a literary magazine, *Cibecue/Dischii' bikoh Magazine*, published by the high school students, the Global Observations to Benefit the Environment international science program that connects students to other scientists and schools via the World Wide Web; Cibecue Watershed Analysis and Restoration Program, a collaboration with the Tribal Planning office, and the ESL and bilingual programs.

The Circle of Learning
Denver Indian Center, Inc.
4407 Morrison Road
Denver, CO 80219
(303) 936-2688
Fax: (303) 936-2699
Lisa Harjo, Director

The Circle of Learning program nurtures children, ages from newborns through age 5, their parents, and families through three initiatives; preschool, home-based instruction, and parent education. The project's culturally based early childhood curriculum, entitled The Circle Never Ends, ensures that developmental needs are met and cultural heritage is preserved. An environmental curriculum is included to influence classroom management and sustain curiosity and interest. The U.S. Department of Education awarded The Circle Never Ends pre-kindergarten curriculum with the Showcase Award in 1989, and a Project Award 1990.

The Family and Child Education (FACE) Schools
Office of Indian Education Program
Washington, DC 20240
(202) 219-1127
Lana Shaughnessy, FACE Coordinator

In 1990, the Office of Indian education created an early childhood–parental involvement pilot program derived from three distinctive modules: the Kentucky Parents as Teachers (PAT), Parent and Child Education (PACE), and the High/Scope Curriculum. The FACE program is implemented in 22 Bureau-funded schools and is currently serving 2,625 Native American parents and their children in the United States. The FACE program assists in the literacy needs of Native American children, ages newborn through age eight, and their parents or primary guardians. The objectives of the program are to prepare young children for school emotionally, socially, and academically. Furthermore, the program encourages parents to engage in lifelong learning by obtaining their GED or high school diploma, for the benefit of preserving and strengthening tribal government, language, and culture.

The Kamehameha Schools
Kapalama Heights
Honolulu, HI 96813
(808) 523-6200
Fax: (808) 537-4214

Founded in 1887, the sole beneficiary of Princess Bernice Pauahi Bishop, the Kamehameha Schools serve students in grades pre-K–12 on their main campus in Honolulu, and two campuses on Maui and Hawai'i. Both the early childhood program and academic curriculum has been recognized for its comprehensive subject matter as well as their focus on the preservation of Native Hawaiian language and culture. Additionally, the schools library houses an extensive collection of Native Hawaiian literature. The Kamehameha Schools support numerous programs that focus on health and welfare, community development, literacy, and Native Hawaiian language and culture. The schools also publish books on Native Hawaiian curriculum and history, and provide financial aid for Native Hawaiians seeking higher education degrees.

Lac du Flambeau Public School
Ojibwe Language and Culture Project
2899 Highway 47 South
Lac du Flambeau, WI 54538
(715) 588-3838, ext. 192
Fax: (715) 588-3243
e-mail: suew@ldf.k12.wi.us
http://www.ldf.k12.wi.us
Margaret (Sue) Wolfe, Federal Program Coordinator

Lac du Flambeau public school is located in north central Wisconsin on the Lac du Flambeau Chippewa Indian reservation. The school provides instruction and sharing of the Ojibwe language, history, and culture, for students in Headstart (pre-K) through Grade 8. Two Ojibwe language and culture teaching assistants collaborate with cultural consultants to enhance the quality of instruction. The program incorporates youth service learning projects into various disciplines such as the Wild Rice project. This project involves a science class cultivating rice to learn the traditional process while fulfilling academic and environment curriculum objectives.

Laguna Middle School
I-40W, Exit 114
P. O. Box 268
Laguna, NM 87026
(505) 552-6466
Fax: (505) 552-9091

The Laguna Middle School is providing numerous learning opportunities through a Four Directions Challenge Grant, which integrates cultural traditions with technology. The project provides learning experiences in video productions, cultural awareness training for its staff, intergenerational activities to stimulate conversation between students and elders, and to design and incorporation of a Keres language curriculum. The project also provides a Laptops at Home program where students who have earned a "laptop license" are permitted to take home a computer evenings or weekends. The Laguna Middle School provides academic opportunities while maintaining the culture and language of their students.

Native American Preparatory School
P. O. Box 160
Rowe, New Mexico 87562
(505) 474-6801 / 421-2270
Fax: (505) 474-6816
e-mail: admnaps2@aol.com
http://www.naprep.org/
Kwen-Lynn Kaleoonalani Kamae Brandow

The Native American Preparatory School sponsors two programs that motivate and nurture the intellectual, ethical, and leadership potential of each student. One program is a five-week summer school program for American Indian junior high students. The other program is a four-year college preparatory school program that merges quality academics and cultural principles. Each of the programs integrate traditional values and identities, rooted in the students' tribal cultures, with Western education to promote lifelong learning and achievement.

Oneida Tribal School
North 7125 Seminary Road
P. O. Box 365
Oneida, WI 54155
(414) 869-1676
Fax: (414) 869-1684
Genevieve Gollnick, Curriculum Director

The Oneida Tribal School, located near Green Bay, Wisconsin, has established a Consolidated Reform Plan, guided by eight components, to enhance the quality and success of the entire school program. Within these eight components (e.g., parental involvement, high expectations for all students, staff development, Oneida language and culture) are descriptions and programs used to meet the needs of the Oneida school community. A part of this plan included the opening of a new school building, designed in the shape of a turtle, that represents one of the clans from which the Oneida trace their ancestry. The Oneida Tribal School is on a path to successfully implement the culture, language, and community of the Oneida people.

Piegan Institute, Inc.
P. O. Box 909
Browning, MT 59417
(406) 338-7740
Darrell R. Kipp

The Piegan Institute, located on the Blackfeet Indian reservation in Montana, supports the promotion and preservation of Native American languages. The Institute, under the direction of Dorothy Still Smoking and Darrell Kipp, developed a Native language immersion program and established several immersion schools on the Blackfeet Indian reservation. Current results reveal that the program has had a profoundly positive influence on Blackfeet youth. There is an increase in academic achievement, positive Native identity, self-esteem, and an increase of young people speaking in their Native Blackfeet Indian language.

Project Tradition and Technology (Project TNT)
Peach Springs School
P. O. Box 360
Peach Springs, AZ 86434
(602) 769-2676
Fax: (602) 769-2412
Philbert Watahomigie Sr., Project Coordinator

Peach Springs School (K–8), the only school on or within 40 miles of Hualapai reservation in Arizona, hosts the Project Traditional and Technology (TNT) program. Project TNT is the recipient of the 1993 Exemplary Programs in Indian Education from the Native American Scholarship Foundation. Two units, the Hualapai Cultural and Environmental Curriculum and the Hualapai Interactive Technology Model, work together to construct the bilingual, bicultural TNT curriculum. The program's success is due to the support of administration, parents, community and tribal governments, opportunities for staff development and training to produce quality instructional materials, increased motivation and attendance, and the results of assessments. In addition, the Arizona department of education, in 1981 and 1983, recognized another Peach Springs School initiative, the Hualapai Bilingual Education program, as one of the most innovative educational program in the state.

Quileute Tribal School
Old Coast Guard Station
P. O. Box 39
LaPush, WA 98350
(206) 374-2061
Fax: (206) 374-9608
http://challenge.uknas.edu/Quileute/Index_4.htm
Frank Hanson, Superintendent

The Quileute Tribal School (K–8), founded in 1979, is located on the Pacific Coast of Washington. The school works to preserve the Quileute language and culture, sustaining a learning environment that integrates the principles of confidence, generosity, courage, and emotional and social stability with western academics and Native knowledge. The Office of Indian Education, U.S. Department of Education, recognized the program as a 1989 Showcase Project.

Rough Rock Community School
Highway 59
RRDS, Box 217
Chinle, AZ 86503
(520) 728-3311
Fax: (520) 728-3216

The Rough Rock Community School, established in 1965, is the first locally controlled Indian school in the United States. The foundation of this school is to assist in preserving the culture and heritage of the Navajo people and to provide quality academic educations. The school has experimented, and found, success in school–community relations, parental involvement, cultural identity, language development, teaching English as a second language, and dormitory living. The school is recognized widely for its production of Navajo language and cultural curriculum materials.

Salmon Berry Shop: A Native Youth Entrepreneurial Project
Nome Community Center, Inc.
P. O. Box 98
Nome, AK 99762
(907) 443-5259
Fax: (907) 443-2042
Douglas McCoy, Executive Director

The Salmon Berry Shop is a consignment craft shop that brings jobs and training to Native Alaskan youth. Under the guidance of an experienced mentor, a Native youth can learn skills in business management, accounting, sales, and public relations. A primary goal of the Native Youth Entrepreneurial project is to promote self-confidence, self-esteem, and life skills to assist youth in staying away from alcohol and drugs. Students are offered other learning opportunities, such as video production, creative writing, and AIDS-prevention training. The Native Youth Entrepreneurial Project has challenged the notion that students who have dropped out of high school are unreachable.

Sand Springs Public Schools Indian Education Program
P. O. Box 970
Sand Springs, Oklahoma 74063
(918) 245-1088
Fax: (918) 241-1916
Mrs. Jerre Brokaw, Coordinator

The Sand Springs Public Schools Indian Education Program was founded in 1977 to provide tutoring for Native students in elementary, junior, and senior high schools. In addition to tutoring services, the program brings culture-related events to other schools, offers college and career information to Native high school students, distributes free school supplies to eligible students, and houses a resource library for the students, community, and school personnel. The program is dedicated to enriching the cultural heritage within Native students while expanding their academic opportunities.

Sherman Indian High School
Wellness Program
9010 Magnolia Avenue
Riverside, CA 92503
(909) 276-6327
Kenneth R. Taylor, Chief School Administrator

Sherman Indian High School currently serves 509 students in Grades 9 through 12, and is located in Riverside, California. The Wellness Program (also known as Wellness Learning Center) assists students in their spiritual, emotional, educational, social, traditional (Native understanding) development. This holistic program helps students to identify and resolve their problems (e.g., substance abuse), and encourages them to focus on their education and complete high school.

Sho'Ban School District #512
Dance of the Salmon Program
P. O. Box 790
Fort Hill, ID 83203
(208) 238-3976
Gloria Osborne, Administrative Assistant

The Shoshone–Bannock Junior–Senior high school is located on the Shoshone–Bannock Indian reservation in Fort Hall, Idaho. The Dance of the Salmon program, a project held annually in summer, educates students in environmental science by identifying environmental factors that interrupt salmon from returning to their Native habitat. Students learn to identify optimum egg incubator densities and configurations, and then test their technology for successful hatching, and increasing egg-to-fish survival at a minimum cost and effort.

Takini Grant School
HC 77, Box 537
Howes, SD 57748
(605) 538-4299
Fax: (605) 538-4315
http://challenge.ukans.edu/Takini/index.html

Takini Grant School (K–12) is located on the Cheyenne River Sioux reservation in South Dakota. The school uses an outcome-based education approach that is multidisciplinary, multiage, and centered on projects and thematic units. Takini Grant School has received state and national recognition for its exemplary efforts to maintain cultural dignity while providing optimal learning opportunities for students and the community. Other courses offered by the school include Parents as Teachers, Early Childhood, and Adult Education.

Tiospa Zina Tribal School
Crawfordsville Road
P. O. Box 719
Agency Village, SD 57262
(605) 698-3953
Fax: (605) 698-7686
Roger Bordeaux, Superintendent

Tiospa Zina Tribal School is located on Lake Traverse Dakota reservation in northwestern South Dakota and southeastern North Dakota. The tribally controlled elementary and secondary school, founded in 1981, addresses the needs of Dakota youth by implementing a community and culture-based education program. The purpose of the program is to nurture the cultural and academic needs of Dakota youth.

Wingate High School
American Indian Science and Engineering Society (WHS AISES)
P. O. Box 2
Fort Wingate, NM 87316
(505) 488-6400
Michelle Eustice, AISES Coordinator

Wingate High School is located on the Navajo reservation in Fort Wingate, New Mexico. Wingate High School American Indian Science and Engineering Society (WHS AISES), provides Native American students with motivation, skills, qualifications, and opportunities in science, mathematics, engineering, community involvement, and postgraduate education. The following are the four components that address the needs of the students: (a) the Math and Science Knowledge Enhancement and Competition component, includes participation in local, regional, and national competitions in math and science; (b) the Community Services component, that includes the Adopt-A-Grandparent program, and McKaffy Clean-Up, Adopt-A-Highway program, Science Mentorship program, and Campus Beautification programs; (c) the Summer program component, that further enhances educational experiences, interpersonal skills, and cultural appreciation; and (d) the College preparation component, that gives students the chance to attend college preparation workshops and conferences.

Yup'ik Arts Festival
Paul T. Albert Memorial School
Tununak, AL 99681
(907) 652-6827

The Yup'ik Arts Festival supports the preservation of traditional Yup'ik arts through intergenerational interactions. As elders and students work collaboratively, the traditional Yup'ik value of respect for elders increases. Heightened community involvement in the arts festival has encouraged non-Native teachers to learn traditional Yup'ik arts, which has increased their awareness of the learning styles of their Native students. The Yup'ik Arts Festival serves as a bridge to promote communication between elders, students, teachers, and the Native community.

NOTE TO THE READER

There are many exemplary pre-K–12 educational programs; the above is a sampling of this powerful movement. For more information and programs, visit our Web site at: http://ed-web2.educ.msu.edu/voice/

Tribal Colleges

Bay Mills Community College
12214 West Lake Shore Drive
Brimley, MI 49715
(906) 248-3354
Fax: (906) 248-3351
e-mail: mmcleod@eup.k12.mi.us
Martha McLeod, President

Blackfeet Community College
P. O. Box 819
Browning, MT 59417-0819
(406) 338-5441
Fax: (406) 338-7808
Ms. Carol Tatseg Murray, President

Cankdeska Cikana Community College (formerly Little Hoop Community
 College)
P. O. Box 269
Fort Totten, ND 58335
(701) 766-4980
Fax: (701) 766-1350
e-mail: sajones@hoopster.little-hoop.cc.nd.us
Scott A. Jones, Director

Cheyenne River Community College
P. O. Box 220
Eagle Butte, SD 57625
(605) 964-8011
Fax: (605) 964-1144
Donna Rae Petersen, Director

College of Menominee Nation
P. O. Box 1179
Keshena, WI 54135
(715) 799-5604, 779-4921
Fax: (715) 799-1336, 799-1308
e-mail: vfowler@menominee.com
http://www.menominee.com
Holly Young Bear-Tibbetts, Director

Crown Point Institute of Technology
P. O. Box 849
Crown Point, NM 87313-0849
(505) 786-5851
Fax: (505) 786-5644
e-mail: jmtutt@aol.com
James Tutt, President
Jay R. DeGroat, Director

D-Q University
P. O. Box 409
Davis, CA 95617-0409
(916) 758-0470
Fax: (916) 758-4891
e-mail: dqpres@aol.com
www.den.davis.ca.us/go/dquaaa/
Christine Tupaz, Director

Din'e College (formerly Navajo Community College)
P. O. Box 126
Tsaile, AZ 86556
(520) 724-6817
Fax: (520) 724-3327
e-mail: fclark@crystal.ncc.cc.nm.us
Ferlin Clark, Director

Dull Knife Memorial College
P. O. Box 98
Lame Deer, MT 59043
(406) 477-6215
Fax: (406) 477-6219
e-mail: rlbear@www.dkmc.cc.mt.us
http://www.dkmc.cc.mt.us/default.htm
Dr. Richard E. Littlebear, Director

Fond du Lac Tribal and Community College
2101 14th Street
Cloquet, MN 55720-2964
(218) 879-0835, 879-0842
Fax: (218) 879-0814
e-mail: statzell@asab.fdl.cc.mn.us
Donna S. Statzell, Director

Fort Belknap Community College
P. O. Box 159
Harlem, MT 59526-0159
(406) 353-2607
Fax: (406) 353-2898
e-mail: pshortman@hotmail.com
http://www.montana.edu/~wwwse/fbc/fbc.html
Dr. Phillip Shortman, Director

Fort Berthold Community College
P. O. Box 490
New Town, ND 58763
(701) 627-4738, 627-3665
Fax: (701) 627-3609
e-mail: ldemaray@nt1.fort_berthold.cc.nd.us
Karen Gillis, President
Elizabeth Yellowbird Demaray, Directory

Fort Peck Community College
P. O. Box 398
Poplar, MT 59255
(406) 768-5551
Fax: (406) 768-5552
e-mail: jimsh@fpcc.cc.mt.us
Dr. James Shanley, President
Margaret Campbell, Director

Haskell Indian Nations University (HINU)
155 Indian Avenue, Box 5030
Lawrence, KS 66046-4800
(785) 749-8457
Fax: (785) 832-6631
e-mail: bmartin@rossl.cc.haskell.edu
Venida Chenault, Director

Institute of American Indian Arts (IAIA)
Box 20007, St. Michael's Drive
Santa Fe, NM 87504
(505) 988-6463, (800) 804-6422
Fax: (505) 988-6273
e-mail: dwarrior@iaiancad.org
Della Warrior, Director

Lac Courte Oreilles Ojibwa Community College
R. R. 2, Box 2357
Hayward, WI 54843
(715) 634-4790
Fax: (715) 634-5049
e-mail: dtrev@win.bright.net
Dr. Minhas, President
David F. Treviranus, Director

Leech Lake Tribal College
Rt. 3, Box 100
Cass Lake, MN 56633
(218) 335-2828
Fax: (218) 335-7845
e-mail: larry@paulbunyan.net
Larry Aitken, President
Jamie Robertson, Director

Little Big Horn College
P. O. Box 370
Crow Agency, MT 59022
(406) 638-2228, 638-7211
Fax: (406) 638-2229
e-mail: janine@maln.lbhc.cc.mt.us
Janine Pease-Pretty on Top, President
Charitina Fritzler, Director

Little Priest Tribal College
P. O. Box 270
Winnebago, NE 68071-0270
(402) 878-2380
Fax: (402) 878-2355

Native American Educational Service College (NAES)
2838 W. Peterson Avenue
Chicago, IL 60659
(773) 761-5000
Fax: (773) 761-3808
e-mail: fsmith#@orion.it.luc.edu
Faith Smith, President

Northwest Indian College (NWIC)
2522 Kwina Road
Bellingham, WA 98226
(360) 676-2772
Fax: (360) 738-0136
e-mail: cshafer@nas.com
Carla Shafer, Director

Oglala Lakota College
P. O. Box 490
Kyle, SD 57752
(605) 455-2321
Fax: (605) 455-2787
e-mail: tshort@olc.edu
Marilyn Pourier, Director

Salish Kootenai College
P. O. Box 117
Pablo, MT 59855-0117
(406) 675-4800
Fax: (406) 675-4801
e-mail: mod@skc.edu
http://www.skc.edu
Dr. Joseph McDonald, President
Michael O'Donnell, Director
Sinte Gleska University

Rosebud Sioux Reservation
P. O. Box 490
Rosebud, SD 57570
(605) 747-2263
Fax: (605) 747-2098
www.sinte.indian.com/index.html
Dr. Lionel Bordeaux, President
Mike Benge, Director

Sisseton–Wahpeton Community College
Agency Village
P. O. Box 689
Sisseton, SD 57262
(605) 698-3966
Fax: (605) 698-3132
e-mail: elden@daknet.com
Gwen Hill, President
Elden Lawrence, Director

Sitting Bull College
HC1, Box 4
Fort Yates, ND 58338
(701) 854-3861
Fax: (701) 854-3403
Cheryl Red Eagle, Director

Southwestern Indian Polytechnic Institute (SIPI)
P. O. Box 10146
Coors Road, NW
Albuquerque, NM 87184
(505) 897-5351, (800) 586-7474
Fax: (505) 897-5343
e-mail: celgin@kafka.sipi.tec.nm.us
Dr. Carolyn Elgin, President
Valarie Montoya, Director

Stone Child Community College
Rocky Boy Route, Box 1082
Box Elder, MT 59521
(406) 395-4334, 395-4313
Fax: (406) 395-4836
e-mail: uanet.425@quest.OSCS.montana.edu
Steve Galbavy, Director

Turtle Mountain Community College
P. O. Box 340
Belcourt , ND 58316
(701) 477-5605
Fax: (701) 477-8967, 477-5028
e-mail: lpoitea@gizis.turtlemountain.cc.nd.us
Lyle Poitra, Director

United Tribes Technical College (UTTC)
3315 University Drive
Bismarck, ND 58504
(701) 255-3285
Fax: (701) 255-1844
e-mail: dmgipp@aol.com
John Beheler, Director

Other Universities and Colleges

Batchelor College
Post Office
Batchelor, NT 0845
Australia
0-89-39 7111, 0-89-39 7100
Fax: 0-89-760 355

Brigham Young University–Hawai'i
55-ZZO Kulanui Street
Laie, HI 96762
(808) 293-3834
Fax: (808) 293-3888
e-mail: Wallace-b@BYUH.edu
Dr. William Kauaiwiulaokalani Wallace III, Director

Humboldt State University
Center for Indian Community Development
One Harpst Street
Arcata, CA 95521-8299
(707) 826-3711
Fax: (707) 826-5258
e-mail: lgr1@axe.humboldt.edu
Lois Risling, Director

Ilisagvik College
P. O. Box 749
Barrow, Alaska 99723
(907) 852-9101
Fax: (907) 852-9102
e-mail: emaclean@co.north-slope.ak.us
Edna Ahgeak MacLean, Director

Lakehead University
Native Language Instructors' Program
Thunder Bay, ON P7B 5E1, Canada
(807) 343-8054
Fax: (807) 346-7746
e-mail: jomeara@cs_acad_lan.Lakeheadu.ca
Wanda White, Coordinator

Montana State University, Bozeman
Center for Native American Studies
2-152 Wilson Hall
Bozeman, MT 59717-0234
(406) 944-3881
Fax: (406) 944-6879
Dr. Wayne T. Stein

New Mexico State University
Indian Resource Development
P. O. Box 30001, Dept. 31RD
Las Cruces, NM 88003-0001
(505) 646-1347
Fax: (505) 646-7740
e-mail: gklineko@nmsu.edu
lanlujan@nmsu.edu
http://www.nmsu.edu/~ird/
Gina Klinekole, Director
Mr. Lance Lujan, Director

Nipissing University
P. O. Box 5002
100 College Dr.
North Bay, ON P7B 8L7, CANADA
(705) 474-3461
Fax: (705) 495-1772
e-mail: chrisj@admin.unipissing.ca

http://www.unipissing.ca
Christine Jenkins

North Dakota Association of Tribal Colleges (NDATC)
3315 University Drive
Bismark, ND 58584
(701) 255-3285
Fax: (701) 255-1844
e-mail: jackb87389@aol.com
Jack Barden, Director

Saskatchewan Indian Federated College
118 College West
Room 118, College West
University of Regina
Regina, SA S4S OA2, CANADA
(306) 584-8333, 584-8334
Fax: (306) 584-0955
http://www.sifc.edu

The University of Waikato
Te Whare Wananga O Waikato
Private Bag 3105
Hamilton, New Zealand
0-7-838-4500
Fax: 0-7-838-4555
Rita Walker

Te Wananga O Aotearo
TE AWAMUTU CAMPUS
1 Factory Road
P. O. Box 151
Te Awamutu, New Zealand
0-7-871-4257
Fax: 0-7-871-3224
David Lewis

University of California, Los Angeles–American Indian Studies Center
3220 Campbell Hall, Box 951548
Los Angeles, CA 90095-1548
(310) 794-9997
Fax: (310) 206-7060
e-mail: champagn@ucla.edu
Dr. Duane Champagne, Director

University of Hawai'i–Hilo
Na Pua No'eau
200 West Kawili Street
Hilo, HI 96720-4091
(808) 974-7678
Fax: (808) 974-7681
Dr. David Kekauliko Sing, Director

University of Montana
Native American Studies Program
600 University Avenue
Missoula, MT 59812
(406) 243-5831
e-mail: craignas@selway.umt.edu
weaselp@selway.umt.edu
Dr. Bonnie Craig, Director
Dr. Patrick Weasel-Head, Associate Director

Higher Education Resources

American Indian College Fund
21 West 68th Street, 1F
New York, NY 10023
(212) 787-6312
Fax: (212) 596-1050
e-mail: bbratone@aol.com
Barbara Bratone, Director of Resource Development

American Indian Higher Education Consortium (AIHEC)
121 Oronoco Street
Alexandria, VA 22314
(703) 838-0400
Fax: (703) 838-0388
e-mail: aihec@aihec.org
Veronica Gonzales, Director

AIHEC Student Congress
P. O. Box 117
Pablo, MT 59855
(406) 675-4800
Fax: (406) 675-4801
e-mail: dana.a.e.grant@skc.edu
Mr. Dana Grant, Director

American Indian Science and Engineering Society
1630-30th Street, Suite 301
Boulder, CO 80301
(303) 492-8658
Fax: (303) 492-3400
Norbert S. Hill

National Institute for Native Leadership in Higher Education (NINLHE)
Office of the Provost
Scholes Hall, 226
Albuquerque, NM 87131-1002
(505) 277-2614
Fax: (505) 277-0228
e-mail: pagoyo@unm.edu
Pamela Agoyo, Director

WICHE–Western Interstate Commission for Higher Education
P. O. Box 9752
Boulder, CO 80301
(303) 541-0200
http://www.wiche.edu
Dr. Ken Pepion

Appendix B

Resources for Native Educators

YOUTH INITIATIVES

Abenaki Indian Center, Inc.
381 Chesnut Street
Manchester, NH 03101
e-mail: abenaki@xtdl.com

Native American and Teens Interested in Volunteer Efforts (N.A.T.I.V.E.) was
started in 1996. This project seeks to educate youth about Native cultures and values such as honesty, integrity, sobriety, and camaraderie. These efforts are accomplished through the encouragement of volunteerism, creativity, teamwork,
community spirit, and leadership skills.

Aboriginal Youth Network
e-mail: tkocnig@ayn.ca
http://ayn-0.ayn.ca/default.htm

The Aboriginal Youth Network (AYN) was established in 1995 by Microworks and
has evolved into an independent, public, nonprofit, charitable organization. The AYN
encourages youth to utilize the Internet as a method of sharing cultures, traditions, and
ideas. The site provides programs, services, youth news, bulletins, powwow listings, art
and literature, events, chat lines, e-mail hook ups, and health sites.

National Indian Youth Leadership Project (N.I.Y.L.P.)
325 Marguerite Street
P. O. Box 2140
Gallup, NM 87305
(505) 722-9176
Fax: (505) 722-9794
e-mail: npniylp@technet.nm.org
McClellan Hall, Executive Director

Founded in 1984, the National Indian Youth Leadership Project, Inc. (N.I.Y.L.P.) is a Native-operated, nonprofit organization based in New Mexico. N.I.Y.L.P. programs apply traditional concepts to contemporary challenges. Currently, N.I.Y.L.P. is working with 30 Native schools and their communities.

United National Indian Tribal Youth (UNITY)
4010 Lincoln Boulevard, suite 202
P. O. Box 25042
Oklahoma City, OK 73125
(405) 424-3010
Fax: (405) 424-3018
e-mail: unity@unityinc.org
http://www.unityinc.org
J. R. Cook, Executive Director
Russell Coker

United National Indian Tribal Youth, Inc. (UNITY), a 501(c)(3) nonprofit organization, offers programs that cultivate leadership skills, instill cultural pride, foster self-sufficiency, and encourage the spirit of unity in American Indian and Alaskan Native youth. UNITY currently supports 168 youth councils in 28 states, which represents more than 12,000 Native youths.

White Bison, Inc.
6755 Earl Drive, Suite 108
Colorado Springs, CO 80918
(719) 548-1000
Fax: (719) 548-9407
e-mail: whtbison@usa.net
http://www.whitebison.org/

White Bison, Inc., is a nonprofit organization that offers youth various Native learning opportunities in leadership training, cultural community change program, and medicine wheel training.

RESEARCH AND DEVELOPMENT

Labriola National American Indian Data Center
Arizona State University
Box 871006
Tempe, AZ 85287-1006
(602) 965-6490
Fax (602) 965-0776
e-mail: iacpae@asuvm.inre.asu.edu
http://www. asu.edu/lib/archives/labriola.htm
Patricia A. Etter, Curator

The Labriola National American Indian Data Center collects and disseminates current and historic information on Native North American tribes, including Alaska, Canada, and the United States. This Center provides a vast array of information on tribal government and history, culture, religion, social life, customs, and biographical information on thousands of individuals. This information is furnished through the use of computer databases, the Internet, and CD-ROM. The center encourages the use of their Web site, which provides current and back issues of their newsletters, publications, and links to multiple Web sites.

Northwest Regional Educational Laboratory (NWREL)
101 SW Main Street, suite 500
Portland, OR 97204
(503) 275-9500
Fax (503) 275-9489
Joe Coburn and Anita Tsinnajinnie

Northwest Regional Educational Laboratory (NWREL) provides research and development in administration, teaching, and curriculum for educators serving Native American students. The NWREL also provides inservice training for school improvement and the prevention of substance abuse.

Pacific Regional Educational Laboratory (PREL)
1164 Bishop Street, suite 1409
Honolulu, HI 96813
(808) 532-1900
Fax (808) 532-1922
Rita Hocog-Inos

The Pacific Regional Educational Laboratory (PREL) is a nonprofit organization supporting educational research and improvement for educators in the pacific. PREL publishes the *Directory of Pacific Professionals for Educational Improvement* to promote collaborative networking and partnership activities. Described in the directory are talented trainers who are dedicated to improving the education of people in the pacific region.

Poutama Pounamu Educational Research and Development Centre
77 Windermere Drive
Tauranga, New Zealand
(07) 544-3581
Fax: (07) 544-0723
e-mail: ted.glynn@stonebow.otango.ac.nz
Mere Berryman

The Pounamu Educational Research and Development Centre supports a variety of education initiatives for Maori youth. The Hei Awhina Matua program works to overcome behavioral and learning difficulties in the home, school, and community settings. The Tuhi Atu Tuhi Mai project focuses on improving writing skills in the Maori language, and the Reading in Maori assessment package promotes reading.

Roger Lang Clearinghouse for Circumpolar Education
Educational and Resource Group
162 Shawmut Street
Chelsea, MA 02150
(617) 884-8405
Fax: (617) 884-8406
Ann Vick-Westgate

In 1987, the Roger Lang Clearinghouse for Circumpolar Education opened its services to collect and disperse successful community and educational programs identified in Alaska, the Arctic, Canada, northern Scandinavia, and Greenland. Results of the collaborations have formed a Circumpolar Curriculum Library, providing resources of culturally and environmentally based northern curricula developed in the late 1970s.

Southwest Educational Development Laboratory (SEDL)
211 East 7th Street
Austin, TX 78701
(512) 476-6861
Fax: (512) 476-2286
e-mail: nfuentes@sedl.org
http://www.sedl.org/
Nancy Fuentes

Southwest Educational Development Laboratory (SEDL) serves Arizona, New Mexico, Oklahoma, and Texas. SEDL develops and disseminates effective research and applications to address issues facing the minority population. Promotion and support of quality education is distributed through training and technical assistance, and is reinforced by evaluation and applied research. In partnership with the University of Arizona, SEDL's current project is focused on maintaining Native languages.

MUSEUMS AND LIBRARIES

Bishop Museum
State Museum of Natural and Cultural History
1525 Bernice Street
Honolulu, HI 96817-0916
(808) 847-3511
URL: //www.bishop.hawaii.org/
Dr. Guy Kaulukukui

The Bishop Museum preserves the natural and cultural history of Hawai'i and the Pacific region. The exhibits include Hawaiian and Pacific artifacts (including Hawaiian royal artifacts), insect specimens, marine and land skulls, plant specimens, marine invertebrate, fish, bird, and mammal specimens. The museum hosts demonstrations, storytelling, and family events. The education program includes outreach and a KIDSPACE discovery area.

D'Arcy McNickle Center for American Indian History
The Newberry Library
60 West Walton Street
Chicago, IL 60610
(312) 255-3564
e-mail: mcnickle@newberry.org
Casey Macpherson

The Newberry Library's D'Arcy McNickle Center for American Indian History was founded in 1972. The library has an extensive collection of history on American Indian tribes. The center provides unique resources to improve the teaching and writing of American Indian history and literature. There are fellowships offered for individual research, summer institutes, conferences, and workshops for secondary and postsecondary educators. They offer reports and research on and by Native people as well as curriculum guides and course outlines. The McNickle center continues its services and updates through the Meeting Ground newsletter.

Hampton University Museum: American Indian Educational Opportunities Program
P. O. Box 6131
Hampton, VA 23668
(804) 727-5981
Fax: (804) 727-5084
Paulette F. Molin, Director

The American Indian Educational Opportunities Program at Hampton University provides scholarship opportunities for Native Americans to pursue their degrees in undergraduate or graduate programs. Research is conducted with unique archival, photographic, and art collections of African American and Native American culture and history.

The Heard Museum
22 East Monte Vista Road
Phoenix, AZ 85004
(602) 252-8840
Fax: (602) 252-9757
http://www.heard.org/
Ann Marshall, Director of Research

The Heard Museum is a private, nonprofit museum established in 1929, promotes the appreciation and respect for Native people and their cultural heritage with an emphasis on the greater southwest and the Native American fine art movement. The Heard Museum sponsors demonstrations, workshops, and lectures from Native peoples, the Native American Fine Arts Resource Guide, and the Annual Guild Indian Fair and Market.

Mitchell Indian Museum, Kendall College
Kendall College
2408 Orrington Avenue
Evanston, IL 60201
(847) 866-1395
Siston Toni

The Mitchell Indian Museum, founded in 1977, maintains a collection of art and artifacts from many northern American tribes (U.S. and Canada). The museum's mission is to promote respect and appreciation of all cultures. Mitchell Indian Museum develops and distributes exhibits and interpretive programs and hosts lectures and demonstrations by regional and national scholars, writers, and artists. Additional resources for education include printed material, loan boxes, videotapes, and filmstrips.

OTHER LEARNING RESOURCES

The Alberta Journal of Educational Research (AJER)
845 Educational Centre South
University of Alberta
Edmonton, AB T6G 2G5, Canada
(403) 492-7617
Fax: (403) 492-0236
e-mail: beth.young@ualberta.ca
Dr. Beth Young, Editor

Alu Like Inc.
Native Hawaiian Vocational Education Program
1024 Mapunapuna Street
Honolulu, HI 96819
(808) 839-7922
Fax: (808) 836-0704
e-mail: nhvep@pixi.com

The Cradleboard Teaching Project
1191 Kuhio Highway
Kapa'a, HI 96746
Buffy Sainte-Marie

D. C. Educational Services
50 Rosser Street
Rozelle Sydney, NSW 2039, Australia
61-02-555-1613
Dianna Chapman

Journal of American Indian Education
Center for Indian Education
Arizona State University
Box 871311
Tempe, AZ 85287-1311
(602) 965-6292
Fax: (602) 965-8115
e-mail: yaqui@asu.edu
Dr. Octavianna Trujillo, Editor

Native Americas: Akwe:kon's Journal of Indigenous Issues
American Indian Program
Cornell University
300 Caldwell Hall
Ithaca, NY 14853
(800) 962-8483
e-mail: bfw2@cornell.edu
URL: http: //NativeAmericas.AIP.Cornell.edu
Dr. Jose Barreiro, Editor

Vision Maker Video
Native American Public Telecommunications
P. O. Box 83111
Lincoln, NE 68501
(402) 472-0483
Fax: (402) 472-8675
Frank Blythe

For further resources, references, and research abstract please visit the *In our Mother's Voice* Web site: http://ed-web2.educ.msu.edu/voice/

Also recommended:

Klein, B. T. (1995). *Reference Encyclopedia of the American Indian* (7th Ed.). West Nyack, NY: Todd Publications.

Crow, J., Crow, M., Knows the Country, S., & Sharp, J. (1996). *1996-1997 Indian Country Address Book*. St. Cloud, MN: American Indian Communication & Information Company.

Contributors

THE EDITORS

Maenette Kape'ahiokalani Padeken Ah Nee-Benham is a Native Hawaiian scholar and teacher. Her patriarchal lineage reaches back to *Pāpā* on the southwest side of the big island of Hawai'i. Her matriarchal lineage is tied to the *ahupua'a of Ka'a'awa* on the northeast coastline of the island of O'ahu. She was brought up to understand that learning was embedded in the family and grounded in Native Hawaiian values and beliefs in the individual spirit and the collective good. Coming to know the self and the world has been a fluid experience for Maenette. She was taught that the world is filled with possibilities and everything holds a promise of intimate knowledge because everything is related. This learning has led Maenette to believe that teaching and learning is holistic, comprehensive, and comparative, and that its purpose is to build strong, positive relationships. Education, then, has a transitional function—that is, it moves an individual from one part of their path to the next. Over time, however, Maenette has observed through her own experiences and those of her cousins that Western education has destroyed Native languages, stories, songs, and "ways of knowing." She observed that many of her Native cousins have not had the benefit of *'ohana* (family), spiritual passion, and a cultural script written by Native people. The work of education for Maenette has come to mean finding a cultural self and a passion and spirit for one's work. It has become her goal in education to build a foundation where Native children can express their full potential.

Maenette has authored numerous articles in the areas of school leadership and educational policy. She is co-author of the books, *Culture and Educational Policy in Hawai'i: The Silencing of Native Voices*, and, *Let My Spirit Soar! Narratives of Diverse Women in School Leadership*, as well as author and editor of the book, *Cases of School Change for K–12 Administrators.*

Joanne Elizabeth Cooper has observed the narrow world she knew as a child growing up in Oregon become a broader, richer place filled with multicultural possibilities. Learning about the world of Native peoples both in Hawai'i and around the world has reinforced her belief that we are all connected to each other and to the land. This knowledge we have much to learn from Native peoples. Joanne believes educators all hold sacred responsibilities to honor each other and work to fulfill the potential in each of us, for our own growth, and for the good of the collective whole. She writes that we are born in community, raised in community, and therefore, must remain in our educational endeavors connected to community and to the "sacred whole." The work of Native education, Elisabeth concludes, is to discover that sacred whole in each child and connect it to the community of peoples who are gone, and those who will come later.

Joanne has authored many articles and book chapters in the areas of organizational change and critical reflection in education, adult learning, and curriculum in higher education. She most recently co-authored the books, *The Constructivist Leader*, and, *Let My Spirit Soar! Narratives of Diverse Women in School Leadership.*

THE AUTHORS—MODEL BUILDERS

Linda Aranga-Low is a K–12 teacher in Auckland, New Zealand. Linda formally worked for the Aorataha Marae as education director. The Marae is a traditional cultural meeting place for Maori. As education director, Linda was responsible for the development and administration of education and training programs for unemployed Maori youth. She worked on the design and implementation of a curriculum employing Maori values and pedagogy. The Marae also housed a *Kura Kaupapa Maori*, a junior school for children ages 1 through 6 , and instruction was conducted entirely in the Maori language. Currently, Linda is a K–12 educator completing her master's degree in education with a focus on Maori education.

Jeannette Armstrong (Okanagan), director of the En'owkin International School of Writing, Canada. Jeannette resides on the Penticton Indian Reservation. A fluent speaker of the Okanagon language, she has studied under some of the most knowledgeable elders of the Okanagon. She holds a degree in fine arts from the University of Victoria. Her visual artistic works have been recognized through awards such as the Mungo Martin Award, the Helen Pitt Memorial Award, and the Vancouver Foundation Graduate Award. She is also a recognized author in Canada. Her published works include two children's books, one of which won the Children's Book Centre's Our Choice award. She has published a critically acclaimed novel, *Slash*, a collection of poetry, *Breath Tracks*, and has collaborated with renowned Native architect Douglas Cardinal on the book, *Native Creative Process*. Her other creative works include producing two video scripts and three poetry–music collaborations.

Jeannette is an advocate of indigenous rights, and was recently appointed to the Council of Listeners on the International Testimonials of Violations to Indigenous Sovereignty. She is an advocate of a healthy environment and social change where peace between all people is a central theme. As a keynote speaker, she has addressed the World Conference on Indigenous Education and the World Council of Churches on Racism in Education, Media and the Church.

Kate Cherrington has been the education director of Te Wananga o Aotearoa, Hamilton, New Zealand. Currently, she is raising her two young children and is working with her daughter's Maori language immersion preschool. Kate's professional skills focus on mentoring and teaching, research, management, and Maori education policy development. Te Wananga o Aotearoa is a Maaori tertiary institution fully recognized and funded by the government of Aotearoa. She is currently active in national reform movements through the Ministry of Education. Her policy work involves aligning educational standards with Maori culture, and also to assure funding of Maori educational programs. Kate is currently studying for a master's degree in educational administration, and has been known to carry out random acts of kindness and beauty.

Genevieve Gollnick, Turtle School at Oneida, Oneida, Wisconsin. Genevieve is currently the curriculum director of the Oneida Nation School (bureau of Indian Affairs grant schools). At the Oneida Tribal School she implements a culture based approach to learning, planning, and evaluation among other school-related responsibilities. Genevieve has also taught Grades 4 through 6. A graduate of Harvard University, she has expertise in the areas of teaching, curriculum, and learning environments. Her professional work includes multiple service projects, professional development, and committee work. Genevieve is a member of the Oneida Tribe of Indians of Wisconsin, and is married with three children.

Paul Johnson has worked in education for the state of Michigan for the past 25 years in a variety of capacities (teacher, curriculum specialist, professional development consultant). He now owns a small consulting firm, Four Directions, that specializes in designing, organizing, and implementing human resource development programs to assist tribal governments, schools, and other tribal organizations. He is an active member of Lansing's Indian community center and is president and chief operating officer of the Lansing North American Indian Center.

Sarah Keahi, Native Hawaiian scholar, The Kamehameha Schools, secondary division, teacher language department, Hawai'i. Sarah has been instrumental in developing a strong Hawaiian language program since the 1970s at the Kamehameha Schools. The Hawaiian language, one of many indigenous languages in the United States, is an official language of the state of Hawai'i, along with English. It is important to note that, between 1966 and 1986, Sarah leads Hawai'i in 'ōlelo Hawai'i (Hawaiian language) and is one of it's few Hawaiian language instructors in secondary schools. There has been a surge in young people desiring to learn the mother tongue which has necessitated the hiring and training of many new Hawaiian language teachers—many of whom are Sarah's former students.

Sarah has served as a president, vice-president, and board member for 'Ahahui 'Ōlelo Hawai'i, a Hawaiian language association. The organization assists and sponsors Hawaiian language publications, workshops for teachers, activities for students, and Native language radio and television programs. She is a member of the Hawai'i Association of Language Teachers, and the Academic Alliance, an organization of second language teachers. Sarah is an advocate of the Hawaiian immersion program, currently in its 11th year in Hawai'i.

Gail Kiernan, Ministry of Justice, Perth, Western Australia. Formally, Gail held the position of Aboriginal Education worker at Lockridge primary school, in the Nyungar language program's education department in Perth,

Western Australia. She coordinated the Aboriginal studies program and worked on counderwriting and teaching an Aboriginal language program. Recently, Gail began an examination of the Indigenous Australian language program, a 4-year certification program, and is actively involved in a language revival, renewal and learning program with aboriginal children and elders. In addition, Gail is forming a language awareness program in a women's prison. She is also active in a variety of community projects focused on the welfare of aboriginal students and their families.

Darrell Kipp, Piegan Institute, Blackfeet Indian Reservation, Browning, Montana. Darrell, in partnership with his colleague Dorothy Still Smoking, heads the Piegan Institute. Begun in 1985, the institute spearheaded one of the first tribal language revival programs for children and adults in north America. This program was showcased on national television and hailed as an exemplary educational and culturally enriching program. Darrell Kipp holds an education degree from Eastern Montana College and Harvard University, and a master's in fine arts in writing from Vermont College.

Rosalie Medcraft is an Aboriginal studies resource teacher, department of education and the arts, Tasmania, Australia. As an Aboriginal studies resource teacher, Rosalie works with teachers in 65 primary and high schools, providing them with professional development in the area of Aboriginal studies. She is also responsible for reviewing, purchasing, and supplying teachers with up-to-date resources, and for promoting the teaching of Aboriginal studies. It was in the capacity of resource teacher that she was a member of a team that wrote the *Aboriginal Studies Guidelines*, which, after being accepted by the education department, is being implemented in Tasmanian state schools. Rosalie is affiliated with the Australian Education Union, the Aboriginal Education Association, and the Mersey Aboriginal Corporation, a nonpolitical community association. She also is an author of several children's books.

L.A. Napier, University of Colorado–Denver, educational administration, college of education. Dr. Napier is a nationally recognized scholar involved in Native education and Native leadership issues. Her writing has appeared in a variety of scholarly journals and she has presented her research at national and international conferences. In her capacity as an assistant professor of education, she teaches graduate-level courses in educational leadership and school law. Additionally, she serves as chair of the American

Indian–Alaskan Native Special Interest Group of the American Educational Research Association. L.A. is also a Kellogg leadership fellow. As a fellow, L.A. designed a professional plan of study that involves the examination of the concept of leadership, with the goal of moving toward a more inclusive understanding of leadership through examination of the values, truths, spirituality, cultural beliefs, and motives that inspire indigenous leaders. The objectives of her work are to identify and study indigenous leaders who have been validated (by their people) as leaders either via elections or by popular opinion, to examine the concept of leadership across diverse situations among indigenous people, and to develop the means to communicate the findings to a wide population via a documentary film.

Kalena Silva is a Native Hawaiian scholar at the University of Hawai'i at Hilo. Born and raised in Honolulu, Kalena has taught at the University of Hawai'i at Hilo since 1984. A firm commitment to the perpetuation of the Hawaiian language and culture has led Silva to study in both Western and Hawaiian educational settings. After graduating from the Kamehameha Schools, Silva earned a bachelor's and master's degree in music, with an emphasis in ethnomusicology, at the University of Hawai'i at Mānoa. In 1989, Silva earned his PhD in music at the University of Washington, completing a dissertation that focused on the comparative musical, linguistic, and cultural aspects of hymn singing by Hawaiians from the islands of Ni'ihau and Hawai'i. He learned traditional Hawaiian chants and dances and graduated in 1973 as a *kumu hula* (hula teacher) from the Halau Hula o Maiki (Dance School of Maiki Aiu Lake).

Silva has performed, taught, and lectured on Hawaiian music and dance throughout Hawai'i, the Society Islands, New Zealand, the United States, Mexico, Canada, and China. He has conducted workshops on Hawaiian spelling an pronunciation using a text he co-authored with Kauanoe Kamana entitled, *The Hawaiian Language: Its Spelling and Pronunciation.* Silva is actively involved in the 'Aha Pūnana Leo (Hawaiian medium preschools) and Papa Kaiapuni Hawai'i (Hawaiian immersion program), serving as board officer, writer, editor, and translator.

Sam Suina is the coordinator of the Indian Education Services Program, Institute for Intercultural Community Leadership at Santa Fe Community College. He has established community based courses, training, and technical assistance related to strategic planning, intercultural collaboration, conflict resolution, and cultural diversity. He holds bachelor's, master's, and doctoral degrees in education and sociology, psychology, and guidance counseling. Sam is a member of Pueblo de Cochiti, where he has served in various official tribal capacities and is the "keeper of the songs."

Susan Wetere-Bryant is director of LIFEworks, New Zealand. Susan is committed to issues of Maori development in education, health, and economic growth. LIFEworks is a research and facilitation consultancy that specializes in Maori projects for government, industry, Maori organizations, and tribal authorities. As one of the few Maori educational providers and consultants, LIFEworks develops programs that empower young people, single mothers, and other disadvantaged groups. Susan brings a wealth of academic and practical experience to this great arena of need. She has qualifications in science, medicine, education, business, and holds a master's degree in educational administration. She is one of the youngest candidates, yet few Maori women have gained her qualifications. Currently, Susan's research and development work is exploring how information and knowledge can best be applied to affect positive change and development. Susan is affiliated with the Association of Social Impact Assessment, New Zealand Educational Administration Society, is a member of the National Working Party's Maori Health Information and Management Committee, and the New Zealand Authors Society.

Miranda Wright is executive director of Doyon Foundation in Fairbanks, Alaska. In this position, Miranda is charged with the task of maintaining open communication and close working relationships with members of 43 Alaskan Native tribal communities. By encouraging lifelong learning, the Doyon Foundation strives to serve the economic and social needs of Alaskan Natives in these communities. To meet these objectives, the Doyon Foundation offers educational scholarships, community coalitions, professional development seminars, and education conferences focused on directing the future of their tribal communities through education and cultural values. Miranda is affiliated with Native Americans in Philanthropy, Council on Foundations, Alaska Interior Native Educators, Keepers of the Treasurers—Alaska, American Anthropological Association, and the Alaska Anthropological Association.

Index